Calling
Men
Out of the
Cave

Calling
Men
Out of the
Cave

Nigel Mohammed

authorHOUSE®

AuthorHouse™ UK
1663 Liberty Drive
Bloomington, IN 47403 USA
www.authorhouse.co.uk
Phone: 0800.197.4150

Scripture quotations are taken from the New King James Version. Copyright
© 1982 by Thomas Nelson, Inc. Used by permission. All rights reserved.

Published by AuthorHouse 01/12/2016

ISBN: 978-1-5049-9249-7 (sc)
ISBN: 978-1-5049-9250-3 (e)

CONTENTS

Acknowledgements

First, I need to give thanks and praise to the one true Living God for his covenant faithfulness to keep me over the last thirty years and whose grace has enabled me to complete this endeavour. Soli deo Gloria

Next I would like to say a big thank you to Esther, my wife. Your belief in me means so much more than you can really know. You add another dimension to the word 'supportive'.

Thank you to my dear friend Brian, his wife and all the Agape Team in Kathmandu, Nepal, who first asked me to write this book- both for The Agape Mission International and helping me to respond to the stirring of the Spirit of God. Thank you Brian for giving me a chance.

The men's group in Worthing that I am a part of has been organic to this project so a big thank you to every one of you and for 'keeping it real'. To John Richards for your friendship, support, depth and wisdom way beyond your years, To Keith in Cyprus, for the connection, To Ric for leading me to the group, To Matthew for your real friendship, love of the Word and authenticity. To Rocky for the changes you have made in your life, to Nigel…keep up with those jokes, I salute you for your achievement. There is so much more to us my brothers than we realise.

Thank you to every man that I have deeply connected with and who knows in a deep place that 'Church' is meant to be so much more. To Marcus in Brighton- my true brother and a great blessing from God. To Wayne my fellow Chelsea buddy whose sharp intellect and ability to be real has always encouraged me.

To Brad and his family in Albuquerque, New Mexico – 'll always love you. Shane in Galveston, Texas for our fellowship in '98, John and his wife Kim in Washington DC for so much love and generosity over the years, To John Hunt in Albuquerque, New Mexico for being the most real down to earth pastor I have ever met… To Brendan my South African brother in Cornwall for your persevering spirit, To Jesse the New Yorker who lives in 'Hicksville', Cornwall for being you. To Howard wherever you are mate, for the fellowship during the nineties, and putting me onto the importance of the Reformation.

Introduction

Walking through the noisy and polluted streets of Kathmandu, Nepal, Brian suddenly turned to me and said 'Its like an Emmaus Road walk'. 'Yeah, I see what you mean' I replied. It was not so much that we were discouraged or downcast as the two disciples, but our hearts burned within us as we talked about what we felt God had called us to. Brian and his wife Ruth had founded The Agape Mission International (TAMI) who rescue women and children at risk and develop leaders. He asked me if I would like to write up on their behalf, a curriculum or a course on masculinity but related to our calling. I later wrote up a six week course and now this book is also a result of that 'Emmaus Road' walk in Kathmandu, Nepal.

I told him that I felt called to speak and minister to the hearts of men, mostly broken men and the effects of fatherlessness and how this prevents men from living out God's calling on our lives. I most definitely did not feel qualified, but he reminded me that God does not call the qualified, rather he qualifies the call.

Chapter one then is about a story of courage that shifts the battle for an entire nation, the courage of Jonathan and his armour bearer as they attempt something outrageous, dangerous and impossible. Jonathan had an abusive, absent and insecure father, so it looks at father absence and its effects, the battles we face today and how both the culture and the Church do not initiate boys into manhood, thus the decline of men from the Church. This means we can learn some things from Jonathan as he calls six hundred men out of hiding in caves onto the battlefield because Church is not a spectator sport.

Chapter two looks at three worldviews and some of the ideologies that have put men under a spell and caused us to live as isolated individuals. Chapter three traces historical father absence in the modern era back to the Industrial Revolution, the importance of initiation rites of passage for boys and young men and the fatherlessness across the twentieth and twenty first centuries.

Chapter four looks at the way that men are called by God to be the foundation of a nation starting in the home, the Church and the community and unpacks some of the key terms related to manhood. In chapter five, I discuss my own personal experience and journey of fatherlessness and how crucial the Father's Embrace and love is. This is the subject of Chapter six and becoming the Beloved of God. Finally, in Chapter seven, in context to the previous chapters, the topic of finding and living our calling is looked at, particularly in relation to our core desires and our true heart, to live in a larger Story *together.*

CHAPTER 1

'They were hiding in Caves'

It was probably the worst military strategy in the whole Bible. Yet it was also one of the most powerful stories of a man who knew his God and what He was able to do and his armour bearer who encouraged him to take a risk of faith, that brought forth a great exploit and victory for the nation of Israel. The definition of an armour bearer is 'An officer selected by kings and generals because of his bravery, not only to bear their armour, but also to stand by them in the time of danger' (Easton's Illustrated Dictionary). It truly shows how we must work together to do great exploits for the Lord Jesus Christ.

Initially there is an estimated three thousand men with Saul (1 Samuel 13v2) but they are reduced to about six hundred men (v15) because the Philistines are operating from a stronghold and terrorizing the Israelites to such an extent that most of the army have deserted (13v7) and *the remainder are hiding in caves.* It is only Saul and Jonathan who have weapons because the Philistines took all their blacksmiths away. The Philistines had 'thirty thousand chariots, and six thousand horseman and *people as the sand which is on the seashore in multitude'* (13v5).

There is a battle to fight, so they are at war; the odds are severely against them but God is with them; they are paralysed by fear and hide in caves and have no weapons; they have no authentic strong leadership and Saul has lost the anointing of God (1 Samuel 15v10-11, 26-28) even though he still wore the crown for another twenty years. David has the secret anointing and will one day be king, but he has to wait another twenty years to wear the crown.

Saul has now become yesterday's man and David is now God's today's man because he has the anointing. Not only has Saul lost the anointing, he is not exactly a great role model of a true father either physically or spiritually. Fathers are essential, for without a father or healthy father figure, a man has no one to facilitate him through the transition from boyhood to manhood.

Israel in these days are helpless, depressed, discouraged and demoralised. They had a man amongst them though, a true initiator with a masculine heart of steel and supernatural courage. Jonathan and his armour bearer step across a line in the sand and attempt something outrageous, extremely dangerous and totally impossible – they try to fight and defeat thirty six thousand Philistines…because they believe that God is on their side. Initially they took out twenty Philistines (1 Samuel 14v14). This was hand to hand combat, blood splattering, bones snapping, voices yelling, swords flying, teeth clenched. And they did it, against ten-to-one odds. Can you imagine what these two men must have experienced *together* in that moment? Camaraderie? Just a bit.

Men can struggle throughout their entire lives to answer the core question of 'Do I have what it takes to be a man' without having been initiated into manhood, and as the man goes, so goes everyone and everything else. I have been like the six hundred hiding in caves, but I have been on a journey that has brought me out, and very simply, knowing that I am a beloved son of the Father has been the way out of my cave to connect with a desire to fight for others which I believe is a calling. This may seem like an oversimplification, it is not, for coming out of our own caves, whatever that might be for us, takes a particular journey.

The people of God in the above scenario are in a very small minority, and this is similar to where Christianity is today. Where are the men in Church? Where are the mentors and spiritual fathers? They are conspicuous by their absence. Much of Christianity in the West (but not all by any means) today is cowering before the enemy (like the six hundred men under Saul) with our entire spiritual arsenal stripped from us because we have compromised ourselves before the enemies of the faith. One of the main reasons why the Church is seen to be so irrelevant today and why it has been pushed to the periphery of society is because of the onslaught of secularism.

The ideological battle – Secular humanism.

Ideas are like the water from a mountain top that trickle downward starting from academia and filtering through society's institutions to eventually seep into the mind of the man on the street. Ideas have consequences then that spread over time penetrating into every crevice of human affairs. These ideas relate also to why men have been stuck in different caves. This book is a call primarily to the Church to invest in men and see that mentors and spiritual fathers are imperative, which means the Church has to become more masculine and it has to create a space and allow men to be very real with each other.

The Apostle Paul in his second letter to the Corinthians states clearly that the real war is unseen because it is a spiritual war. 'For though we walk in the flesh, we do not war according to the flesh, for the weapons of our warfare are not carnal but mighty in God for the pulling down of strongholds, casting down arguments and every high thing that exalts itself against the knowledge of God, bringing every thought into captivity to the obedience of Christ' (2 Corinthians 10v3-5). Any ism is an ideology. Secularism is therefore a demonic stronghold, an argument that exalts itself against the knowledge of God in creation, Holy Scripture and Jesus Christ.

Secularisation is the sociological process and secularism is the philosophy that underpins it. The Oxford Dictionary of Sociology defines it as follows:

'Secularisation is the process whereby, especially in modern industrial societies, religious beliefs, practices, and institutions lose social significance...The secularisation thesis maintains that secularisation is an inevitable feature of the rise of industrial society and the modernisation of culture. It is argued that modern science has made traditional belief less plausible; the pluralisation of life-worlds has broken the monopoly of religious symbols; the urbanisation of society has created a world which is individualistic and anomic, the erosion of family life has made religious institutions less relevant' [1]

This is quite comprehensive in its effects, for it filters into all human affairs. Secular humanism in particular has effectively kept the Christian faith in the private sphere and not allowed its influence in the public arena. This cultural landscape needs to be painted with broad strokes to understand its historical context and relevant underlying ideologies; we will look at this in chapter two.

Dr Patrick Sookhdeo the International Director of The Barnabas Fund, a charity which represents and fights for the persecuted Church worldwide states that

'The attitude of Western opinion-formers to Christianity and Christians has been summarised by the term 'Christophobia'. It is demonstrated in the gradual restriction by Western states of the right of Christians to freedom of conscience. As a result, religious freedom in the West is shrinking,

---

[1] Gordon Marshall, Oxford Dictionary of Sociology (Oxford University Press, 1998) p.588

and intolerance towards Christians has become par t of Western culture. This trend is so strong that the European Union would not even allow a reference to the Christian heritage of Europe in the draft Constitution of the European Union, which was finalised at an Inter-Governmental Conference in December 2003'. [2]

Western culture, particularly Britain, has a great Christian heritage; maybe Western governments are deluded by a kind of collective but selective amnesia? What is needed today are new heroes of the faith who are willing to do great exploits like Jonathan by taking great risks in faith. The Lord Jesus invested in twelve men, so he started small, trained, released and empowered them. Men are therefore crucial to the advancing of the Kingdom of God, yet men have been in serious decline from the Church as we shall see from a Tear-Fund survey at the end of the chapter. It is time to Awake.

Moreover, an historic Father Absence in the culture that is now of epidemic proportions and the lack of authentic mentors and spiritual fathers in the Church keeps men in various types of 'caves'. When a man has no father or father figure to secure him in his masculine identity, the man abdicates his true destiny to various substitutes including looking to the woman to define his nature and purpose. Yet only authentic masculinity can bestow masculinity and so initiation rites of passages which are universal and have been practiced for thousands of years were abandoned by Wester n culture with the onset of industrialisation, when men effectively left the home.

We have battles to fight, we are at war (it is the backdrop to the whole Bible) and the odds can seem against us in

---

[2] Dr Patrick Sookhdeo, *The Way Ahead, returning Britain to its Christian path* (Barnabas Fund, 2010) p.23

what has become a Babylonian pagan culture whose national leaders are thoroughly secular and relativistic. It has long been believed that in the West we now live in a Post-Christian era and not just because a German philosopher declared that God is dead (Nietzsche). When a nation sells its Christian heritage for a bowl of relativistic soup, then the ancient gods rise again in different forms and strongholds of the enemy take a firm foothold.

Father Absence is a spiritual issue

The warfare passage in Ephesians 6v10-18 follows the imperatives for family relationships in chapter 5v22-6v1-4. To destroy a nation, the enemy has progressively destroyed the family, especially across the Twentieth Century and into the

21st, and most importantly there has been a demonic assault on *manhood* and *fatherhood*. The battle for masculinity and fatherhood is a spiritual one and until the culture and the Church acknowledges both that Fathers are absolutely essential and the Church acknowledges and responds to the spiritual nature of father absence, then we will kept numb by the depth of our denial.

The Culture and the Church have ignored how essential fathers are for way too long. Consequently men are hiding in caves of addiction and have been taken out from their true calling in a whole variety of ways. There is an Old African proverb that says *'If the young men are not initiated into the tribe they will burn down the village....just to feel the heat'.* Why do they burn the village down? Because they are angry and men in Western culture have been conditioned to believe that all anger is bad, and so men have not known how to process their anger that stems predominantly from a generational and pathological father-wound.

Despite their desperate situation, Jonathan and his armour bearer had courage, crazy, outrageous, unspeakable courage of deep heroic proportion. Jonathan must have known he was loved with a love not of this world because perfect love casts out fear (1 John 4v18). Also he had a deep close friendship with David, the man who was emerging as the true king and who had the anointing of God (1 Samuel 16v13). God can heal the father wound in us and He can initiate us into Christ-like masculinity; I will talk about my own journey in chapter five, but intimate relationship with God that penetrates our whole being and genuinely close friendships with other men is so desperately needed because men tend to not get very real with other men. We have to reverse this trend.

Jonathan's father was absent

So we see that in 1 Samuel 14v1-2 that Jonathan was not fathered very well by Saul. *'Now it happened one day that Jonathan the son of Saul said to the young man who bore his armour 'Come let us go over to the Philistines garrison that is on the other side. But he did not tell his father'.*

Why did Jonathan not tell his father? He probably would have laughed at him and destroyed his faith. Saul was very insecure, jealous, immature and self-absorbed. He did not offer any strong healthy masculine strength to his son; if he did Jonathan would have been able to confide in him about his desire to do a great exploit for God.

This is core to this book, the effects of father absence on men, but how God can heal and initiate us into connecting and living from our masculine core, and coming into our destiny. It means being Christ-like, so crucial to this is integrating and seeking to balance both the Lamb and Lion qualities of the Lord Jesus Christ. Western culture does not teach and initiate boys and young men into connecting with their masculine core. In my experience of over twenty five years, the Church does not seem to either. As a fatherless man I drifted aimlessly for over twenty years self-protecting in a cave of isolation and various addictions, but God came for me, initiated me and took me on a journey, but more of that later.

Mentors, spiritual fathers and initiation rites of passage are needed.

This is a call primarily to the Church then to be very intentional about raising up mentors and spiritual fathers in our communities, to show fatherless boys, youth and men that God can Initiate and Father us where we have not been fathered. The Church needs to see how crucial it is to alleviate the pandemic of fatherlessness by practicing initiation rites of passage for young men and indeed to father un-fathered men.

This transition into manhood and the community of men by mentors and fathers has to become the norm in both the culture and the Church because initiation rites of passage are not only of historical and of universal relevance, but Jesus himself had to separate from his mother at the age of twelve because that was the cultural norm (Luke 2v43-50). Furthermore, there is a Scriptural pattern when God's Word would come to a man but then He would work *in* them for many years before he worked through them and brought them into their calling and destiny. This was a form of initiation.

Although men tend to carry their burdens alone, we need to know who the people are in our lives that we can share vision, goals and calling with, without being ridiculed or disregarded. Jonathan knew though who he could go to. He goes to his trusted armour bearer and begins to share his plan. This opens a question for us; 'Do we know who our trusted armour bearers are? Or 'Are we prepared to be someone else's armour bearer for a season'? In verse 6 of chapter 14 of 1 Samuel, Jonathan says *'Come let us go over to the garrison of these uncircumcised; it may be that the LORD will work for us. For nothing restrains the LORD from saving by many or by few'.*

This seems to lack wisdom and discernment, for even Peter before he stepped out of the boat onto the stormy fierce waves said 'If it is you, command me to come to you on the water' (Matthew 14v28). Peter usually acts quite impulsively but this is about *extreme* discipleship and it means that before Peter gets out of the boat, he had better make sure that Jesus think's it's a good idea. However, Jonathan knew his God.

If Jonathan was operating from a Western mind-set of scientific probability, predictability and empirical evidence, he would probably be one of the six hundred hiding in caves, because he would want to be in control and because of fear. But this is Jonathan and he knows his God, and 'the people who know their God shall be strong and carry out great exploits' (Daniel 11v32) Jonathan steps out in extreme, radical faith because he knew what God was able to do. Many are afraid to step out in faith unless they have a sure 'word from the Lord'. At this point in the story, Jonathan did not even have a sure word from God. All he had to go on was what he knew God was able to do, that's it. What this shows also is that God is not necessarily with the majority.

Now the Philistine army were numbered at an estimated 36,000 (1 Samuel 13v5) The men of Israel who were with Saul were about 600 men as mentioned, and they were hiding in caves (v22). So that leaves 2 against 36,000. Insurmountable odds? Depends on our view of God. Jonathan looks at the Philistine army and effectively say's to his armour bearer 'I think we can take them'. In the natural realm it will result in certain death. The only possible edge against such odds is maybe the element of surprise and yet Jonathan seems to destroy even the element of surprise by his 'strategy'. *'If they say to us 'Wait until we come to you, then we will stand in our place and not go up to them. But if they say 'Come up to us, then we will go up for the LORD has given them into our hands; and this shall be a sign to us'.*

Although in the natural this seems insanely suicidal and like the worst military strategy in the Scriptures, it depends on how you look at it. It is breathtakingly courageous faith to walk into the face of absolute certain death and yet take the risk...all because he knew what God could do. However great our vision is though, we need to have the right kind of men at our side. Jonathan's armour bearer's response in verse 7 is crucial

'Do all that is in your hear t. Go then; here I am with you, according to your heart'.

This also speaks volumes for the armour bearer who is not even named in Scripture. He could have said 'Do you have a death wish or what? or 'Have you completely lost the plot'? But he is with him all the way. Great things can happen when men have friendships of this depth and commitment, it makes the difference between just getting by in our caves of mere survival, anger, rage, addictions, uncertainty, passivity and indifference or living the adventure with God on the cutting edge.

Basically *the whole nation* of Israel reaped a great blessing and victory simply because the armour bearer encouraged Jonathan in what he felt stirred to do. How important is it to have even one close friend we can bear our soul with, to encourage each other in what God is stirring us to do for Him? Saul and his army were literally *stuck* in caves of fear and discouragement with the enemy attacking on every side. But now the balance of war is about to change because of the exploits and courage of one man and his armour bearer. Jonathan and his armour bearer are not average men. For average men need a much bigger sign until they move out in such great faith and courage.

So these two fiercely courageous men *crawl* up on their hands and knees up a hill against an army of 36,000 to obvious annihilation....in the natural. God is looking down from his throne, watching these two guys crawl up the hill and thinking 'You have got to love these guys'. Well you have to don't you?

The power of stories

Bad news travels fast, but really good news travels faster. After Jonathan and his loyal friend the armour bearer took out about twenty men, the Angel of the LORD shows up and knocks down the entire Philistine army. *A story starts to spread.* The story spread so rapidly from the mountain top down into the valley and into the fields, to the nation. Everywhere the Philistines are trembling because fear has gripped their hearts and then the earth itself came into agreement as it were, at the same time and trembled and quaked. The entire demonic realm that inspired the worship of false gods trembled – the atmosphere totalled changed and the battle shifted....because of the courage of just two men.

There is power in stories

Men need great stories. Today's generation of men in the western world are a generation of men without stories, we don't know who we are, why we are here or where we are going. David Murrow in talking about 'teaching and the masculine spirit' states that

> *'For centuries men have learned heroism and self – sacrifice through great stories, which they stored in their hearts as boys. If we want our young men to be courageous followers of Christ, we must tell them stories of people following Christ courageously. We used to tell the stories of martyrs and missionaries*

to our boys. Now we don't. Young men see Christianity as a religion, not an adventure' [3]

Let us see the results on two groups of people of the outrageous courage of Jonathan and his armour bearer.

In verse 21 of 1 Samuel Chapter 14 the story of courage that infiltrated the Philistine camp brought some Hebrews to their senses. It awakened them, and do we not need our true masculine hearts to be deeply awakened?. Here are Jews dressed like Philistines. They talk like Philistines because they picked up their language. They worshipped the gods of the Philistines and served in their army against Israel, which meant that they served and lived for the purpose of seeing Israel annihilated. The story of the courage of two Hebrews *awakened* and penetrated to the *hearts* of these Hebrews who were hiding as Philistines in a Philistine persona. But something was called to the surface and they could no longer pretend to be Philistines. We need something from our core to be called to the surface and to live instead of merely survive.

They began to take off the Philistine costume and weapons. 'What am I doing' they must have asked themselves. This is not who I really am. They abandon the position of fighting against the purpose of God and they make a beeline to the frontline of the battle and turn to fight against the demonic horde of Philistines. Why did they do this? They just heard a story, but a story of courage. It is only the story of courage that speaks to the seed deep within and reminds people who they really are. Every town and city has people who once confessed the LORD who now live for things opposed to Him.

Now verse 22 describes those who are still in the land but *hide* from any personal accountability, personal sacrifice and from any demand put on their life. They are neutral and

[3] David Murrow, *Why Men Hate Going to Church*, (Nelson Books, 2005) p.179

missing in action. They want all the benefits of the Kingdom but do not want to pay the price. They do not live with a passion for obedience, or a passion to know and love God. They are apathetic, lethargic, and complacent. *They are hiding in caves when there is a battle to be fought.* As they say in the military – the men are 'missing in action'.

Human Extremity – The meeting place with God

Jonathan, though he had an abusive insecure father, crawls on his hands and knees with his armour bearer, against an estimated 36,000 Philistines, as numerous as 'the sand on the seashore'. This is another dimension of Extreme. God is not always with the majority, in fact he usually starts small and works through individuals and experiences of such extremity that if God does not come through then we are done for. This should be the normal Christian life where we need God *desperately*, but Western culture worships a life of comfort, predictability and control. Do we *really desperately need* to pray 'God give us this day our daily bread'?

In the West we have been seduced into believing that a life of material comfort with all the latest technological gadgets represents 'the good life'. Yes but it is life without having to depend desperately on God. Too much comfort, too much consumerism, too much exposure of the mass media, anaesthetizes, hypnotises and numbs us. This especially keeps men in different kinds of caves far from their true calling to live in a larger story of adventure with God. The Scriptures show us that human extremity is frequently the meeting place with God.

Losing everything can be the very thing that we need in order to face our self as a man and dismantle the walls of self- protection we erect. Jonathan's situation is so extreme that if God does not show up then he is dead. God called Abraham to 'Come out of Ur' and to leave everything he was familiar with and go out into the unknown. Have we 'Come out of Ur'? Have I?

True Christianity is not meant to be a spectator sport, but 'men' like the six hundred sit in Churches week after week, month after month, year after year. Spectators missing in action and passive......until they hear a story that awakens their true noble heart and reminds them 'I was not born to simply occupy space, I was born to advance a Kingdom, to take ground back from the powers of darkness, I was created to make a difference to history, to be a history maker'. Do we even want to be history makers? Men like Jonathan and his armour bearer are needed today. Men whose hearts God has been stirring, to penetrate into the core masculine but buried hearts of men. In short, mature mentors and spiritual fathers able to truly disciple, counsel, heal, envision, engage in warfare and who are connected to their own core masculine hearts and who know Abba Father deeply, intuitively and experientially.

Jonathan and his armour bearer call men out of their caves onto the battlefield

So the story of courage brings the 600 men from the mountains of Ephraim out of their caves...to the front-line of battle. Why? Because that is who they *really are*, but it took a man who remembered and knew deep in his spirit what God could do, even though he had no guarantee that God would intervene. He had no prior 'word from the Lord'. He is going into a battle he cannot naturally win and will mean certain death, based on '*maybe* the Lord will work for us'. This is not a statement of doubt, it is simply acknowledging that God knows best, but even if he is being presumptuous, God does not seem to mind, it is certainly better than being fearful and running away. The battle for a whole nation is shifted because a courageous man who knew his God took a risk, a monumental seemingly crazy risk agreed, but as it has been said – faith is spelled r-i-s-k

'Courage is almost a contradiction in terms. It means a strong desire to live taking the form of a readiness to die. He that will lose his life, the same shall save it. This paradox is the whole principle of courage, even quite earthly or brutal courage. He can only get away from death by continually stepping within an inch of it…he must seek his life in a spirit of furious indifference to it, he must desire life like water and drink death like wine' GK Chesterton.

Where do you get courage like that? From knowing in your deepest being that you are delighted in and are the joy, the treasure, the delight, the apple of your Fathers eye. It realigns and reorients our whole being; something is shifted in us at a deep place. Whether this comes from your earthly father or from God himself, we all need this. However, to even get to a place of acknowledging our need takes a certain journey. This is especially so for men in Western culture because we are conditioned to be so self-sufficient, independent and to not engage our emotions. Therefore because of this conditioning and a variety of major upheavals and changes historically and also because of the father wound, men shut down and are blinded by the denial of the how deeply the arrows of their wounds have really penetrated.

Tragically, this crucial affirmation and love that is imperative to set our hear ts free to live fiercely and courageously very rarely comes from deeply engaged fathers because of the arrows lodged so deeply in their own hearts. Hence a generational father absence characterises and underpins Western culture that goes back at least to the Industrial Revolution in modern times anyway. We all have a calling on our lives whether we believe that or not, but the message from the arrows that have wounded us keep us stuck in certain ways.

Maybe one of the tests of authentic manhood is when a man goes into a battle, any battle, he is not sure of winning but he goes in anyway because he knows in his core that it is the right thing to do. This implies that if men are to be awakened to who they really are, who God has made them and called them to be, then we have to come out of hiding from the numerous 'fig leaves' we put on and from the variety of caves that we retreat to.

We must not walk alone

To come out of hiding we need each other and must not walk alone. Men need to have a sense of belonging to a small group of true brothers and be connected to a bigger network. This will help to reduce feelings of isolation and depression. So are we willing to find the peer support and establish a small group of men who are tired of their cave and want true camaraderie? Here we can be safe to be real instead of put up with pretence. In a small group we can share our experiences and stories, increase communication, and engage in activities that enable us to get our true hearts back. Jesus started small, invested, trained and released men, so we have a proven model that is sustainable.

This is where the analogy of the Cave is poignant because we isolate ourselves either to lick our wounds or become victimised by them, or simply bail out and go passive and become a spectator. There are way too many 'Spectators' in the Church, especially men. In his excellent book *'Sons of the Father'* Gordon Dalbey in a chapter entitled 'The wolf loves the lone sheep' refers to a well-known Christian leader who fell to sexual immorality. He quotes a friend he used to work with

> *'He (the leader) was so afraid of looking bad that he just would'nt open himself up to any other man'. Dalbey continues 'And so,*

instead of risking looking bad to one or two Christian brothers-who presumably could have ministered mercy and healing, he fell to temptation and looked disgraceful before the merciless millions of men in the world – who were grateful for yet another 'hypocrisy-in-the-church' excuse to avoid meeting Jesus' [4]

Whatever is un-confessed stays in the dark and the enemy has a foothold where there is darkness. Unless we bring our secrets, our deepest wounds and everyday battles into the light of the grace and truth that is in Jesus, through true koinonia (fellowship, common-unity) there is a high probability that we will stay in our own caves where our various 'fig leaves' remain intact. We have to be prepared to reveal the 'man behind the mask' and a committed small group can provide the context for this.

What does the story of Jonathan and his armour bearer say to us?

There are some things that *stay hidden* in the absence of the stories of courage, in the absence of strong fathers, and in the absence of very close brothers we have camaraderie with. Authentic, strong masculine identity that initiates and offers wholesome strength and sacrificial love are some of the essential masculine qualities that stays hidden. The qualities of being willing to first die to self and lead by having a vision larger than himself and being an agent of change in the home, family, church, local community, wider society and the world is also what stays hidden. However, the capacity to carry and apply life affirming energy can only be formed in sacrificial love of fully engaged fathers who know that boys have to separate from the mother in order

---

[4] Gordon Dalbey, *Sons of the Father,* (Kingsway, 1996) p.100

to find, develop and be initiated into their manhood by the community of men.

Consequently, real intentional and proactive love gives us the courage to be real and free from having to put on a mask, and free to live boldly in a bigger story. This makes Jonathan even more amazing because he had such a self-indulgent, immature, and profoundly insecure and abusive father who had also lost the anointing of God. In short, Saul's leadership was carried out in the flesh. We need to focus in on Saul a bit here because it will help us to see that men do not hide in caves when there is a battle to fight for no reason at all. It does not happen in a vacuum. The tragedy of life is not death; rather it is what we allow to die in us while we live.

Why did these six hundred men hide in caves?

Samuel the prophet had already warned the people of the *behaviour* of the king who would reign over them in 1 Samuel chapter 8v11-18, but they insisted in having a king reign over them 'that we also may be like all the nations'. Then in chapter 9 we see that Saul's father Kish was a powerful and wealthy man. From 9v3-10 Saul comes across as a rather passive peasant with a servile personality even to his own servant. He is it would seem under the dominance of his father. He does not have strong presence in chapter 9. The dominance of his powerful father would have prevented him from developing his own uniqueness as a man and therefore the seeds of his insecurity were sown. Insecure people in positions of authority can do profound damage-despite the sovereignty of God.

The character of King Saul

In 1 Samuel 15v10 the word of the LORD came to Samuel 'I greatly regret that I have set up Saul as king, for he has turned back from following Me, and has not performed My commandments'. And it grieved Samuel, and he cried out to the LORD all night. In a moment the kings authority was taken from him. It was over. He remained in office and even wore the crown for another twenty years but the anointing was removed. Pretty scary really, that God removed his anointing and yet allowed him to stay in leadership. However, that is no guarantee of authority. A position can give a man power, but authority comes from character that has been developed through years of hard preparation. It comes also from obedience and from God's anointing. Floyd McClung in his excellent little book *The Father Heart of God* says

> 'A closer study of the life of Saul reveals a pattern, a terrible, unmistakable pattern of inferiority and emotional hur t, independence, pride and the fear of man. I call it the Saul Syndrome'. [5]

He goes on to state that in 1 Samuel 15 the characteristics of Saul's unresolved inferiority are pointed out – stubbornness and independence (rebellion is as the sin of witchcraft and stubbornness is as idolatry v23) pride (Saul went to Carmel and indeed he set up a monument for himself v12). The fear of man (I have sinned because I feared the people and obeyed their voice v24) and disobedience (Why then did you not obey the voice of the LORD? To obey is better than sacrifice v22). The Saul Syndrome Floyd McClung says is like a cycle that Saul got locked into. Inferiority led to > independence which led to > pride. Pride led to > the fear of man which led to > disobedience and this is underpinned by > inferiority.

Saul's deeply unresolved issues led him to so manipulate and control others that his domination of those under him was virtually unbearable. It is no wonder that the four hundred

[5] Floyd McClung, *The Father Heart of God* (Kingsway Communications Limited, 2001) p.105

men who joined David much later in Adullams Cave (1 Sam 22v1-2) were 'in distress, in debt and discontented'. Saul seemed to live in fear of his father, and the chasm in his soul was filled by such inferiority and self-doubt that he controlled others to the point of being abusive. As a victim of father absence he then victimised others including of course his own son. Therefore this father wound is generational, it repeats itself. Unless the father wound and its effects are honestly faced and truly recognised, men will continue to be blinded by their denial and stay stuck in a variety of caves.

The Father wound in men.

The last passage in the Old Testament (Malachi 4v6) is about fathers and sons and so God in his Word conveys the truth of the father wound. It is significant that the promise of Malachi 4v6 both in its promise and its warning frame the very doorway to the New Covenant, in other words, the threshold to the coming of the Messiah. This text also implies that the brokenness in this world between children and fathers reflects the brokenness between humanity and God. In short, the restoring of relationship with the Father is, in fact, the very focus of God's saving power in a fallen world.

So Jesus came to reconcile humanity to the Father (John 14v8-13) and nowhere in the world is the impetus for that reconciliation more keenly felt than in relationship with our earthly fathers, both for men and women. This father wound in Malachi 4v6 is the difference between what our dads have given us and what Father God wants to give us. Every man and woman therefore bears the sting to a greater or lesser degree of the father wound.

Men experience it very differently though because only masculinity can bestow masculinity. No pain penetrates more deeply into a man's heart than being abandoned emotionally and/or physically by Dad, and so no pain therefore more directly beckons and needs the saving power of Father God.

This is why the eschatological vision of Malachi 4v6 focuses directly on healing this wound.

It is also why the enemy of our souls is literally hell-bent to make us deny in any way he can not only the father wound itself, but also the very Fatherhood of God. Only women can articulate their own father wound and how that affects them.

However, for men, this is most emphatically not about an academic theory or a theological perspective from a detached ivory tower. This is a debilitating crippling injury and reality, a pathological wound which just for starters renders us men inadequate with the woman, deeply distrusting of other men, distorted in our image of God, especially the Father Heart of God, and therefore cut off from our destiny to be true noble warriors, lovers, mentors, prophets, kings and priests.

The father calls forth the core masculine qualities in his son, historically through initiation rites of passage, which have long since been abandoned by Western culture. So without this essential input from our fathers as boys, we cannot later really see ourselves as deeply masculine and so the chasm between our underlying inadequacy and who we really long to be as a man, fills with shame. Our spirit cries out for a truly committed father, whether we acknowledge this or not and without other men who have walked through the rough terrain into God- designed authentic manhood, our cry echoes in the darkness.

The father of lies

Therefore a different father, the father of lies enters in and promises to cover our shame and inadequacy through a variety of compulsive and addictive behaviours, from drugs, to pornography, to work-aholism, to religious legalism. The list of 'fig leaves' in how we cover this deep father wound is very long. Indeed the fig leaves are inevitably of an addictive nature. Gerald G. May states in Addiction and Grace

'I am not being flippant when I say that all of us suffer from addiction. Nor am I reducing the meaning of addiction. I mean in all tr uth that the psychological, neurological, and spiritual dynamics of full-fledged addiction are actively at work within ever y human being. The same processes that are responsible for addiction to alcohol and narcotics are also responsible for addiction to ideas, work, relationships, power, moods, fantasies, and an endless variety of other things' [6]

Only the dignity of true son-ship can overcome the shame of abandonment, therefore surely the task for Christian men, particularly leaders, is to redeem and restore manhood to its true created vitality and only those who have had their own father wounds healed and been able to live as truly liberated, healed beloved sons of the Father as Jesus did, can then mentor and spiritually father other men.

Moreover, only these types of men can align their hearts in such a way, that they will be able to transcend the denominational divides in the Church. As I said, the father of lies gets us to ignore or deny this father wound. How many men had fathers who taught them about their sexuality when they became a teenager? In my experience, it is such a shocking minority, that it is no wonder that men tend to visit on society the very prophetic curse of destruction of Malachi 4v6.

How do you kill a living organism such as a plant? Two ways.You can either physically beat it and smash it up. There is another way. Just leave it alone. Don't water it. Either way it dies. Abandonment kills. So wounded un-fathered men have been projecting onto the world, the deadly impact of father abandonment, from the sheer amount of single parent

---

[6] Gerald G. May M.D. *Addiction & Grace* (Harper & Row Publishers, San Francisco, 1988) p.3

mothers, to abortions, sexually transmitted diseases, to rioting, violence, domestic abuse, woman-hating lyrics, to criminality, addiction, etc... it goes on and on. To only punish the behaviour, the symptoms, does not solve the problem. Men have to be helped to lie still, while the Surgeon cuts out the infection, the toxicity of the father wound. Ask men in prison or gangs what kind of father they had. This takes a journey to be real, down to the bone real with each other and with God.

Therefore, insofar as Christian men shrink back from facing the father wound, we abdicate to the world our sacred calling to model and proclaim the true Father of all, the God and Father of our Lord Jesus Christ. It is a wound of absence, so it needs presence, father presence, yet they are not available, so this is where true mentors and spiritual fathers can lead broken men through the journey of facing their wounds not avoiding them. Mature mentors and spiritual fathers encourage us along the path of processing our buried repressed emotions and not deny how we really feel, help us to grieve, to weep, to facilitate us as God opens up our hearts to attend to the buried pain, and who can point us toward our true destiny – so we can say with Jonathan 'Come let us go, it may be that the Lord will work for us'. He will.

We men (and women) therefore need to be very intentional about dealing with our emotional wounds so that we do not get locked into a similar cycle or the 'Saul Syndrome'. Such was Saul's insecurity that even when everyone knew that Jonathan his own son was the real hero (as well as his armour bearer) he wanted to kill his own son simply because he ate some honey and disobeyed him.

This is unimaginable insecurity and jealousy. Fortunately for Jonathan the 'men' who had come out of the caves had caught some of Jonathan's courage and stood up to Saul (1 Samuel 14v43-45) and so he did not die. This was the kind of 'man', the kind of 'leader' that the six hundred men who were hiding in caves were under. This may help to explain how Saul must have affected these men, for they were also dominated by their fears. As a man goes so goes everyone else including those under his authority.

So Jonathan was hardly fathered well, but it speaks volumes for the kind of man he was that he had such a relationship with God that instilled in him a fierce warrior heart of indescribable courage and leadership. It speaks of the depth of his spiritual maturity. He loved David deeply and his father wanted to kill his best friend, yet he remained faithful to his father even unto death on the battlefield (1 Samuel 31v2-6) It implies that his friendship with David and his relationship and *heart* understanding of God were able to form such courageous and masculine qualities in him despite having such an abusive father.

It provides real hope for un-fathered men. Jonathan's relationship with God, his close friendship with David and his armour bearer, and having a cause to live for that was greater than himself were factors that contributed to him being forged into such an exceptional tender warrior.

Lamb and Lion – Jesus is the model for true manhood.

This term 'tender warrior' resonates with the Lamb and Lion qualities in Jesus who is both of these and we are called to be conformed to the image of God's Son. A man needs the support from a band of true brothers as well as fathers, to be able to balance these qualities of lamb and lion. Too much lamb and you get a weak, effeminate, passive man, too much lion and you get a macho fool unable to feel and be real. The key is finding the right balance. So men need the right kind of mature mentoring and fathering to develop their bold courageous masculine side as well as their soft tender caring side.

What this really says about Jonathan is that no matter how bad we had it, no matter how damaging our father was, no matter how deeply buried our true masculine hearts are within us, no matter how 'taken out' we are by our own past or the huge shifts in the culture, God can and longs to father us where we have not been fathered and we can have a small group of men to be real with. In short the Father is running to us to embrace to and bring us into the fullness of our sonship and adoption.

Much of Christianity in the West as I have mentioned is like the six hundred men in caves is also cowering before the enemy with our entire spiritual arsenal stripped from us because it has compromised itself before the enemies of the faith. In 1 Peter 3v15 God tells us to 'always be ready to give an answer (defence) to everyone who asks you for a reason for the hope that is in you'. When was the last time someone stopped you to enquire about the reason for the hope that is within you?

Maybe a friend grasps you by both shoulders, looks you squarely in the eye and pleads 'You have *got* to tell me, what is the reason, where do you get such inspiring hope'? The problem is that no one ever asks. Why? Have the hearts of men in the Church become buried beneath a kind of sanctified resignation that masquerades as patience or something else? This is not to generalise, there are always exceptions but people are not exactly ripping the roofs off Churches to get in.

Men and the Church

If men with the courage, vision and sheer audacity of Jonathan and his armour bearer, are rather rare in Church, then does Church put men off, does it turn them away and create an assumption that Christianity is only for particular types of men, or even only for women and children? What is the situation with men and the Church today in the West?

Statistics published by Tearfund a Christian development charity, conducted by Christian Research (www.whychurch. org.uk/gendergap.php) show that men have been in decline from the Church. In a recent twenty year period, 35% of believing men have left the church, 70% of boys raised in the Church leave by their mid- teens or early twenties, 25% of Church going women attend Church without their husbands, and perhaps the most serious of all, 49% of men under thirty have left the Church in the last twenty years.

This last figure is serious because men under thirty are in their prime and need adventure, battle, challenge, to be tested, to be initiated, and need to live for something worth dying for. I myself never found these essential outlets to express my own emerging masculinity in the Church and God himself initiated me through driving me into a long painful wilderness and began to father me. I will dedicate a whole chapter to my own story later on, but the point is nearly half the men under thirty have given up on the Church.

This Tearfund survey reveals a 65/35 gender split in the church in the UK, which means that Church is predominantly a *feminine* environment. Moreover the recent trend shows that this gender split is increasing. At the current rate of loss it is predicted that by 2028 men will all but have disappeared from the Church in the UK. Furthermore research carried out by Focus on the Family in America suggests that if a child is the first person to become a Christian, there is only a 3.5% probability that the rest of the family will follow. If the mother is the first to become a Christian, the probability rises to 17%. However, if the father is the first, there is a 93% probability that the rest of the household will follow.

This is the effect of a man's influence and the obvious conclusion being that if you reach the men, you reach the families. Men are essential, it's really that simple. To reach men though, you have to enter their world and be intentional about creating a masculine environment that will attract men. Judaism and Islam are overtly masculine, and although

Christianity on the outside looks masculine, on the inside it's more feminine.

Boys need to separate from the mother in order to become masculine, this is built into us as men, we have to separate from the mother or our masculinity development is arrested. If the Church is feminine, maybe unconsciously men in the culture sense this and assume that Christianity is only for women and children, or even for particular types of men. So men have clearly rejected the Church because there is no space to express their masculine energy. The way we do Church clearly needs to be more masculine.

Why have the above Stats occurred, what is happening? These questions have to be asked.

The Church does not initiate boys into manhood

If 70% of boys raised in Church leave by their mid-teens or early twenties, and 49% of men under thirty have left Church in the last twenty years, then leaving Church has become a sign of manhood, because they are not initiated from within Church culture, so boys and young men seek manhood-validating experiences outside the Church, This is serious.

David Murrow in an article *'Boyz to Men'* states that

> *'Throughout human history men have had the sacred responsibility of initiating boys into manhood through rites of passage. In primitive cultures the men abduct the boys from their mothers and take them into the wilderness. There the boys learn the ways of men. Religious secrets are revealed. Initiates are subjected to tests and ordeals to prepare them for manhood. These rites of passage are often strenuous or brutal… Once a boy passes these tests he's returned to the village and his manhood is publicly recognised in*

elaborate ceremony... Have you noticed how many of the heroes of our faith were driven into the wilderness and tested by God? Scripture is full of these tales: the flight of Jacob; the exiles of Moses and David; the temptation of Jesus. Today's Church (and our larger society) no longer formally recognises manhood' [7]

Can you see what is actually happening both in the Church and in Western culture? For thousands of years, religion has provided boys with initiation rites of passage, but since we no longer do this as a Church or a culture, boys have created their own rites of passage. Leaving Church becomes a sign of manhood; just as in gang culture serving a prison sentence is a sign of recognition or even honour, just like getting an 'ASBO' is a badge of honour (Anti-Social Behaviour Order) for young boys in deprived inner city areas or poor council estates. It is way overdue that men began taking responsibility for initiating boys again.

The men of the Church must provide boys with a vision of manhood and show them that pursuing Jesus Christ does not emasculate our manhood, it does not feminise us, rather following Christ takes us on a journey to live with a greater more substantial strength as God breaks the walls of the self-protection of the false self we construct. He will heal the father wound, initiate us and crystallise a calling out of our time in the desert. God will work in us to help us balance both the Lamb and the Lion qualities in Jesus, so that we become authentically masculine (humble before God, fierce against the enemy, and real with each other) and genuinely tender (more feminine) and carry an authority forged out of our brokenness and time in the wilderness.

---

[7] David Murrow, *Boyz to Men article* (www.churchformen.com/boys/boyz-to-men/

This topic is an entire book in itself, but men need to communicate a vision of biblical Christ-like masculinity, because the Church has been haemorrhaging men for decades. Both Secularism and Islam have proven their ability to capture the hearts of men, whereas frankly the Church has allowed itself to become too feminised.

The decline of men from the western Church cannot be denied then, and this is a big topic that takes in the huge panoramic view of two thousand years of Church history, it is not my intention to try this. I am addressing the story of the courage of Jonathan and how it changed the battle in favour of the people of God and why men are hiding in a variety of caves, largely through a pathological father wound and the abandonment of initiation rites of passage. I am saying that men cannot live out of a deep fierce life enhancing place without a community of men who are intentional about exploring unresolved issues in themselves and the problems in the culture and the Church.

This is not to judge but I became intentional about wanting to live in a bigger story and pursue a sense of calling, and I had to let go of some things that got in the way in order to ask Jesus to give me my heart back, because so much of it had been frozen in time, buried. That, as well as God initiating me through a long wilderness experience (chapter five). If the story of Jonathan and his armour bearer does not stir men's hearts to go and find where they lost their hearts and to find their position in the huge battles we are currently facing in the West, then this will not be of any interest to you. Then you won't want to try and find a cause to live and die for – to leave a legacy behind you.

Through my own journey of initiation and becoming proactively engaged in the process of becoming a beloved son of the Father, what has been the most overarching issue is that there is no reproducing of mature disciples who live courageously for Jesus and no spiritual fathers.

This resonates with two of the deepest needs for men that I am addressing; we need a band of brothers and spiritual fathers.

The lack of mentors and fathers in both the culture and the Church implies that men have lost their way, how did this come about?

CHAPTER 2

Under a Spell 'I could not remember my true self'.

In C.S.Lewis' sixth story in the Narnia series '*The Silver Chair*' we read of two schoolchildren summoned to Narnia to find the missing prince of the kingdom. Long ago in the past the prince was abducted by a witch and placed under a spell, taken to her underground kingdom and chained to a Silver Chair. Every day for about an hour or so he would awake from the spell, realise where he was, *who* he was and where he came from. Under a spell, Prince Rilian lost all recollection of who he was and where he came from. Toward the end of the story, the children free the prince from the chair and the power of the spell. After hearing that he had been under the spell for ten years, the prince says

> '*For now that I am myself I can remember that enchanted life, though while I was enchanted I could not remember my true self*' [8].

Everyone has a worldview: Ideas have consequences

An idea about reality is the same as a worldview. Any worldview is a basic set of assumptions that attempt to answer questions such as: Where did the universe come from? Who are we? What is right and wrong? Imagine trying to complete a jigsaw puzzle without the box-cover. It would

---

[8] C.S. Lewis, *The Silver Chair* (New York: Harper Collins, 1994) p.164

take a long time to finish it because there is no *objective* yardstick to explain where the individual pieces fit.

So if two people trying to complete the jigsaw puzzle only had their opinion of where the pieces fit, and said 'What is true for you about where the pieces fit is not true for me' then they might just take a long time to complete it not to mention be very confused. They would have to try and do their best as they went along but it would be a real struggle. What makes a jigsaw puzzle make sense is the box-cover. It is the box-cover that helps us to know where the pieces fit into the big picture. A worldview is like a jigsaw puzzle in that it helps us to explain how it fits into the real world as it really is.

While the Prince was enchanted he could not remember his true self, in other words his true identity, and human identity is an essential part of a worldview. This succinctly describes the way that many men feel today; we cannot remember our true selves or true identity because we have been under a spell....of ideas. This is where 'the spell' began-with ideas that progressively got rid of the box cover that explained reality. If our belief about the world corresponds with the world as it really is, then it is true because truth must correspond with reality in order to be credible and valid.

Water from a mountain top trickles down

Obviously water that trickles from a mountain top is heading downwards heading for the streams on the ground where everyone can access it. Ideas are like the water from a mountain top that trickle downward and have consequences that spread over time penetrating into every crevice of human affairs. They penetrate vertically into every sphere of life, shaping the values, social structures and institutions of a culture. Ideas normally begin and develop as religious doctrine, abstract philosophies, or scientific theories and then permeate downward into music and the arts.

The ideas then become institutionalised into a society's laws, politics, social and economic structures, before finally flowing into popular culture and affecting the lifestyle of the average 'guy on the street'. Today the guy on the street believes for the most part that he is either the result of random chance of million or billions of years of evolution, or he has a 'pick and mix' belief by drawing from several 'box-cover' ideas of reality.

For example today's belief about Political Correctness is based on the worldview of Relativism. So this box-cover presupposes that morality and truth are relative and that moral absolutes do not exist and that we must have *tolerance* for all beliefs. In a speech by the politician Michael Howard, the leader of the opposition at the time, gave an example of a father of four who had chased a gang of vandals with a rolling pin for his own protection because they had just smashed his shop window, was bound over to keep the peace and charged with carrying an offensive weapon. The victim of the crime becomes criminalised because the human rights of everyone are more of a priority than justice.

Human beings have a conscience, and this is how the Creator has left His mark on us despite our insistence to make up reality according to ideas that are independent of Him. He won't be totally ignored, hence our conscience. We know that this law that charged the victim of the crime has departed from all human reason and common sense. Hence some clichés carry some truth…'political correctness gone mad'. It is insane because it calls good evil and evil good; it reverses what the Creator has instilled into creation. This is what has happened with men to some extent in the second half of the twentieth century when Human Rights became the dominant issue and in particular Equality of gender roles but it has left men in confusion about what makes them *distinctive.*

To argue that men and women are exactly the same in every way is to check out of the Hotel Reality because physically and in other ways we are blatantly different. Men are called to initiate and the woman responds. This is built into our makeup by the Creator. Which box-cover of reality, of human identity do men base their masculinity on though? Relativism says gender is...relative (there's a surprise!) and what you want it to be? Is murder absolutely wrong or relatively wrong? We tend to still believe that murder is absolutely wrong, but the box-cover of reality has changed and so the perpetrators of blatant crime also have the same Human Rights as the victim. Box-covers (worldviews) change over time because human society itself is always changing.

The reason why men have been 'under a spell' and forgotten their true selves is because of the changes in the belief system of western culture, but this applies to any culture at any time. As noted above, a worldview can be described as a set of assumptions held consciously or unconsciously in faith about the basic makeup of the world and how the world works. Assumptions are basically what we presuppose and consider to be true. For example we all assume that $2+2=4$ and we don't question the truth of it because it is a mathematical law.

Everyone asks questions and believes something about the origins of the physical Universe, the physical world, what human beings are, what is right and wrong, knowledge, whether there is a God or not and where is history heading. Although everyone asks these same basic questions, the answers they give are radically different. The way that people and societies answer these questions determines the types of cultures and societies they create. Some answers to these questions lead to poverty and barbarism; others lead to development and civilisation. Although ideas/worldviews spread over time – today with modern information technologies, ideas require less and less time to spread – for good or ill.

The goalposts have moved – and how the water trickled downwards.

From the first century up until something called the Age of Enlightenment in the 17th and 18th centuries, the dominant worldview (box-cover) in the West presupposed that an infinite personal and eternal God created the entire universe both animate and inanimate, spiritual and physical. The universe is separate from Himself but not independent of Him. God is both transcendent meaning outside of His creation and immanent meaning present within it. Because God is everywhere present and immanent in history, the universe is not a closed system, it is open to God's purposes and intervention. This was the overarching worldview known as *Theism* which allows for and believes in communication and interaction between the physical and spiritual realms. God has revealed Himself then in creation, Holy Scripture and ultimately in Jesus Christ.

The period after the Middle Ages is known as 'The Enlightenment' as mentioned because of the revolutionary scientific and philosophical ideas that challenged the previous medieval religious worldview. This Age of Reason challenged what it viewed as irrational superstition and *it changed the face of western culture.* In fact, the goal posts not only moved, they emigrated because man tried to get rid of God.

The general consensus about God began to disintegrate in Europe and England during this Age of Enlightenment. Philosophers sought to free man from religious dogma and doctrine and also to set human beings free. God began to take a back seat and the huge shift for this was called *Deism* which believes that God is *only* transcendent but not immanent (near or present), not involved in history and the physical world. Deism as a worldview believes that 'God' created and founded the universe on natural laws. God was seen as the Great Clockmaker who wound up the universe and left it to run on its own laws and run its own course. The universe was believed to be a machine with man at the centre.

Because God is not immanent and involved in his creation, then he can't reveal himself in creation, so his revelation is excluded. This means that human beings cannot know him *personally* despite being able to use their reason to grasp his existence. Thus the goalposts moved again but they moved even further downward into Atheistic materialism and *Secularism* and this is how the waters changed as they trickled down the mountain over time. There was a spiralling downward then from Theism to Deism and then Secularism.

If God cannot communicate with mankind and is not involved in his creation or history, then why do we need God at all? The revolt against the Biblical view of God that began in the 'Age of Enlightenment' (to liberate man from the 'Dark Ages') to set humans totally 'free' to decide and interpret reality for themselves was nearing completion by the end of the 19th and start of the 20th century. In addition to this, other Post- Enlightenment thinkers such as Karl Marx, Sigmund Freud and Friedrich Nietzsche compounded this atheistic presupposition of reality and of human beings.

Indeed these thinkers in their own way laid the foundation for 20th century secular humanism. *Man was now alone in an impersonal and mechanical universe.* Secularism as a worldview permeated every area of life and materialism became the dominant worldview of the West. Human beings were now 'free' from all absolutes and able to decide what is true and false, right and wrong. This is how and where the waters of ideas have trickled down the mountain, human beings believe that they are free now to make up reality as they see fit.

What about the Church?

In terms of how the Church reacted, perhaps another simple mountain analogy may help. Imagine a small Swiss mountain village which represents the Church but there is an avalanche of snow coming down a mountain at breakneck speed threatening to bury the village. The avalanche of snow represents the worldviews of Deism, Atheism and Secularism and all their related cousins. The people in the village run for their lives but some stay and are overtaken and swamped by the avalanche. Secularism basically split society into 'public and private' spheres.

Faith was removed from the public arena and was privatised. The Church was simply not equipped to deal with the avalanche and so the 'fundamentalists' took to the hills and became radically separated from the 'world' and the 'liberals' embraced secularism to the point where the miraculous in Scripture, the deity of Christ, the inerrancy of Scripture and the character of God all came under attack and were severely compromised by the liberals.

So instead of engage and defend the Biblical worldview as able to explain all reality in a way that corresponds and is liveable and pragmatic, the Church effectively disengaged from all that it considered to be 'secular' and retreated into a ghetto of what it defined as 'sacred'. Darrow L Miller states

> *'Thus many believers suffer from 'split personalities'. Their lives are divided into compar tments: the 'religious', what they do when attending church or a Bible study; and the 'secular', their jobs, recreation, and education. Millions of believers operate from this worldview, which I call evangelical Gnosticism. Never hearing the challenge to be consciously Christian in their daily lives,*

they are conformed to the pattern of this world and have secular minds' [9]

Christians have unwittingly absorbed and assimilated the worldview of ancient Greece in particular in that it divides the universe and heaven into the 'spiritual eternal' realm which they considered as 'sacred' and the physical world of mankind was seen as 'secular'. This sacred/secular divide are the waters that have trickled into the Church from the culture. Everything that comes under the category of 'Christian' then is implicitly believed to be 'sacred' and everything outside the Church is implicitly viewed as 'secular'.

The professionalization of the pastoral ministry.

One of the most blatant ways that Christians have been secularised is through the professionalization of the pastoral ministry. John Piper writes

> *'We Pastors are being killed by the professionalizing of the pastoral ministry'. He continues 'The world sets the agenda of the professional man; God sets the agenda of the spiritual man. The strong wine of Jesus Christ explodes the wineskins of professionalism. There is an infinite difference between the pastor whose heart is set on being a professional and the pastor whose heart is set on being the aroma of Christ, the fragrance of death to some and eternal life to others'(2 Cor 2v15-16)* [10]

---

[9] Darrow L. Miller, *Discipling Nations* (YWAM Publishing, 1998) p.46
[10] John Piper, Brothers, *We are not professionals* (Christian Focus Publications, 2003) p3.

If the world sets the agenda of the professional man, it is the worldview of secularism and this is how the Church in the West has insidiously been rendered so ineffective in it's mission to be salt, light and a city on a hill, because of this sacred-secular divide.

The professionalism of the 'ministry' has effectively created two peoples of God rather than one, because ministry has been defined by what the pastor does, or by what those in 'full time' ministry do. This has been the case throughout most of Church history. The idea that a select few are called to minister to others needs to be challenged, because there is no 'clergy-laity' division in the New Testament, for just as God is Trinity yet One, so also the people of God although diverse with various functions, are one.

All believers are called initially to Someone and then to participate in God's mission as witnesses of his saving grace to the whole of society with everything that entails. The Church needs to recognise, support and equip people for ministry in the home, the school, college, the workplace, the neighbourhood, the community and other spheres of influence. The existing assumption of 'ministry' results in people's everyday lives being separated from the communal life of the Church. There has to be a uniting of authentic New Testament theology and practice in a way that transcends 'professionalism' that encompasses all of life. In short, a theology of the people, for the people and by the people.

So New Testament ministry which simply means 'service' is cut off from God's purposes in the market place, the home, school, college, the work place. Going into 'the Lord's work' then means going into some kind of 'full time' ministry like a pastor, youth worker, or missionary instead of being co-workers with God in his creating, sustaining, redeeming and consummating work in both the church and the world. What is needed is a comprehensive biblical foundation for the Christian's life in the world as well as the

Church. This would imply a 'total ecclesiology' that has no 'clergy-laity' division.

'Full time' professionalised ministry by those trained and educated theology keeps people passive, dependent, and ill- equipped for life in the world.

This professionalism is also overtly Middle Class and but it can result in a very *subtle* concept of 'Niceness'. So the implicit message is created that Christian men are 'nice', respectable and conform to social conventions of acceptable etiquette and language. Paul Coughlin writes

> *'Think about 'nice' people in your life, then ask yourself, for instance: Do they stand up to injustice? Do they fight against what they know to be untrue? No. They don't have it in them. 'Nice' can't confront this world's pain, the way Jesus did and commanded us to do as well...somehow we have mistaken niceness for righteousness, when the Bible says that the righteous are as bold as lions'* [11]

This is not to critique the middle classes and make assumptions that reveal more of *my* issues than objective facts, but there are very few working class Pastors in today's western church and this professionalism keeps men in Church way too passive. So an insidious secular mind-set that sets the agenda for 'ministry' effectively emasculates men from being proactive, courageous, dangerous, bold risk takers that engage and impact their communities and offer life giving energy. Also it fails to produce men who know they are at war and refuse to go on this journey alone because it produces a 'get them in and keep them in' kind of ghetto mindset, whereas Jesus trained and released men.

---

[11] Paul Coughlin, *No More Christian Nice Guy* (Bethany House Publishers, 2005) p.20

Men can feel then that there is nothing required of them in Church culture, that there is nothing that creates the space to express core masculine qualities like being appropriately dangerous, bold, taking risks, and having a challenge that stretches them to the limit. That is maybe why historically, sport basically took over from the Church where men are able to express certain traits of masculinity including raw emotion, for in certain types of Church culture it is social conventions of acceptable language and respectability of what many men conform to.

A culture of professionalism and dominant middle class effectively anaesthetizes men from knowing that they are even at war and add a bit of individualism into the mix and we become like the men dropped behind enemy lines with no weapons and on our own. How long would men last if this really happened in a physical war? We must be intentional about not living as isolated individuals because it is very easy to assimilate the culture's lifestyle.

We are called to live distinctive lives

In their thought provoking work on contemporary Church entitled 'Total Church', Tim Chester and Steve Timmis state that

> *'The New Testament word for community is koinonia, often translated by the now anaemic word 'fellowship'. Koinonia is linked to the words 'common', 'sharing', 'participation'. We are the community of the Holy Spirit (2 Corinthians 13v14) in community with the Son (1 Corinthians 1v9); sharing our lives (1 Thessalonians 2v8), sharing our property (Acts 4v32) sharing in the gospel (Philippians 1v5; Philemon 6) and sharing in Christ's*

suffering and glor y (2 Corinthians 1v6-7; 1 Peter 4v13)' [12].

Men are called to initiate the sharing of our lives, particularly those in leadership but how can you carry a cross professionally, or weep professionally, or carry in the body the death of Jesus professionally, or be persecuted professionally, be a professional clay pot, or become the refuse of the world professionally? Leaders must not be detached, they must be visible and live their lives openly in the midst of the believing community, which means being real with their own sin and brokenness. This is something that 'professional men' can find difficult to do.

The waters of ideas from the mountain leave humans on their own

The hollowness of secularism leaves humans alone and dehumanised in a mechanical universe and one of the 'fruits' of this worldview is individualism; where today in the West the individual is king and so some individuals try to 'juggle' many activities and responsibilities including family, friendships, career, leisure, decisions, money, relationships etc. From time to time the pressures overwhelm us and so we drop one or more of the balls we juggle and church can become one of these balls. However church is not meant to be just another ball we juggle. At the centre of true community or koinonia is not 'me' as an individual but 'us' as members of the Christian community and decisions of significance we make together.

The way we do Church then can be subtly more individualistic than truly communal in sharing the whole of our lives. Consumerism is another member of the family of

---

[12] Tim Chester and Steve Timmis, *Total Church, a radical reshaping around gospel and community,* (IVP, 2007) p.41

secularism and can cause Christians to 'consume' worship so that it becomes subtly about how it affects us as individuals rather than communal. Ideas then have consequences but how does this relate to men forgetting who they really are? Individualism only serves to compound the way men isolate and do life alone. It keeps men in caves of passivity who tend to live for 'thing's or sport, sex, anything to numb the thought that to quote Jack Nicholson 'What if this is as good as it gets'? Into the 20th and 21st century, these ideas that changed the box-cover of reality has created a *silent* epidemic of fatherlessness.

CHAPTER 3

Historical and Social reasons for Father Absence

The Industrial Revolution

The twentieth century and the first decade of the twenty first have been characterised by a tragedy of father absence, but the disappearance of fathers began long before the twentieth century. Ultimately, the roots of fatherlessness and the fundamental orphan spirit that marks us to a lesser or greater degree goes back to the Garden of Eden. However, the roots of father absence in the modern era can also be traced back to the Industrial Revolution during the early 18th century because it had such a radically damaging effect on fathers and sons, and this has continued right up until the present. It is a generational fatherlessness.

The cost of Industrial 'progress' to the lives of men was and still is virtually ignored, it changed practically every personal and social relationship men had. It is debatable that the most profound impact of the Industrial Revolution was on the father- son relationship. Industrialisation was and is inseparable from father absence and the abandonment of initiation rites of passage. Several writers on men's issues trace the disappearance of the father-son bond and it's critical and damaging effects to the monumental transition from an agrarian culture to an industrial one.

This is not to imply the pre-Industrial times were the halcyon days as a benchmark, but it caused a paradigm shift in this essential relationship between fathers and sons in particular. For boys would spend all day with their fathers outside learning their trade, so there was separation from the mother, transition into something new and incorporation into a new maturity, which are all traits of initiation rites of passage.

The Industrial Revolution took men away from working the land, so they lost touch with the earth and the wholesome stewardship of it. It took men away from their families and sons. Boys then grew up in a predominantly female environment and had no or very little masculine presence in which to model manhood. Technology began to dominate and machines took over human life.

Time became money, so the natural rhythms that came with working the land disappeared and the factory clock and machines began to rule men's souls. It caused deep alienation in terms of men's identity which came from the fathers teaching the sons their trade by spending all day with them. From working the land in an extended family where men were initiated into manhood by their fathers, men's bodies and souls became *enclosed* in factories.

This enclosure of men alienated them from each other, it changed the relationship of older men to younger men because no longer did the older generation see themselves as teachers or mentors to the young. This was catastrophic. Life became a competition and it became mechanised, including men. It also caused alienation between a man and his work, for before he created, made, invented, produced and saw the fruits of his labour, but working in factories men never produced anything that had their own individual stamp on it, so there was nothing to express who he was or what he believed in.

Furthermore men and women were alienated from each other for they no longer worked together to accomplish the daily tasks necessary for survival. Ever since the Industrial Revolution boys have had to develop a masculine identity in the absence of male role models and so a predominant mechanistic way of life became the basis for men to define themselves. Men became enclosed in factories and dominated by machines.

Andrew Kimbrell in his extensive work 'The Masculine Mystique' states that the industrialised male faced a grim new reality.

> 'First, his land had been taken from him, enclosed for use by the large landowners for export crops. This enclosure violently cut him off from his traditional life, community and work. Next he himself had been enclosed into the foreign environment of the industrial workplace, most often for six days a week, twelve to sixteen hours a day. Virtually all of his waking hours were spent away from his family and the natural world'. [13]

The Industrial Revolution was based on the market mechanism of Capitalism – supply and demand and this was one of the ideologies and strongholds of ideas that put men under a spell that resulted in them living in isolated cocoons.

Western society therefore became deeply disconnected from nature. But with men becoming so horribly enclosed in the factory system, they also became disconnected from their bodies and emotions. So men began to retreat into their intellectual hideouts, or shut down emotionally because the disappearance of Initiation rites of passage emasculated men. For there was no one to help them through the difficult transition from boyhood to manhood. Men and masculinity itself had to be re-created in the machine's image if the epoch of industrialism was to succeed.

Initiation rites of passage have been of universal significance historically, however with the coming of the Industrial Revolution western culture abandoned them

---

[13] Andrew Kimbrell, *The Masculine Mystique, The Politics of Masculinity* (Ballantine Books, 1995) p.38

because of industrial 'progress'. The wildness and fierceness in men that would protect and give life was kept buried, and this wildness and fierceness is also about daring to be vulnerable and transparent among other things, to come out of hiding in our caves, to put aside our frail little egos and coping strategies to manage and control life and to get into the battle.

The necessity of male initiation

Rites of passage have always been part of human history and are universally embraced. Many of us will have participated in ceremonies associated with rites of passage such as baptism, graduation, marriage. Even the journey from baby, to child, teenager, father, grandfather, elder, and death are rites of passage. Western culture does not define them as such any longer.

Rites of passage have three stages, *separation* which is separation from the present; *transition* where we learn new skills, ways of being, gain knowledge, we change and seek a new future. Finally, *incorporation*, when we recognise that we have changed, we are no longer how we used to be and we act accordingly, and others also recognise the changes in us. The rite is defined by the lesson we have to learn in order to make progress.

Indeed Christian baptism is a rite of initiation for in it we enter into a deep union with the death and resurrection of Jesus. In defending masculine initiation rites, David Thomas notes that

> 'Christianity is based upon a stor y of sufferings, followed by resurrection, redemption, and ascent into a better life

that is an uncanny parallel of the narrative
enacted in almost all ritual initiations' [14]

Although the Church does not seem to teach this, it is a shame because the whole mind-set of initiation characteristic of baptism would help us to make sense of our own sufferings, it would provide a framework to absorb our pain into a larger sense of meaning. Pain and birth are inseparable both in nature (the death of winter and the new birth of spring) and in our own life as humans, for growth and maturity involves change that is painful, but which births us into the next stage of our life.

As I have mentioned, as far back as the Industrial Revolution in the early18[th] century there have been no clear and definite Initiation rites of passages from boyhood to manhood for men. If father absence is such a deeply rooted problem and if manhood today needs to be redeemed and restored, it begs some crucial questions to be asked such as

'What is the root of man's wounded-ness'? 'What is authentic masculinity'? 'How can authentic masculinity be restored'?

The root of man's wounded-ness

Although the onset of industrialisation radically changed the relationship between fathers and sons, the true root of men's wounded-ness and of course women's brokenness as well, is the historic Fall of man in the Garden of Eden because a fourfold alienation occurred. Humans became alienated from God, from them-selves so experienced a division within as men and women, from each other so conflict between men and women began here, and alienated from the environment, so human labour and the raising of

---

[14] David Thomas, *Not Guilty; The Case in Defence of Men* (New York: William Murrow and Company, Inc.) p.57

the next generation would be marked by toil and hardship, not that work per se was a curse, it was not for it came before the Fall, but now it will be marked by alienation.

This alienation is marked essentially by self-consciousness. In his Science Fiction novel *Perelandra* C.S.Lewis portrays the tempter as offering Eve, the Green Lady, a mirror in which she can see herself. He tells her:

> *'That is what it means to be a man or a woman-to walk alongside oneself as if one were a second person and to delight in one's own beauty. Mirrors were made to teach us this art'*[15]

So instead of being God-conscious and living for his glory as image bearers, man became *self*-conscious. Next, Adam and Eve feared, then hid from God because they were afraid to be seen naked. Fear of exposure then hiding, next they blame and feel shame. These are the roots of all human psychology and so we all have our own fig leaves to cover our deep sense of fear, shame, inadequacy, guilt, and painful alienation as human beings.

Men in Western culture tend to be rational, independent, and faithless and do life alone because they are not wired relationally in the same way women are. These are sophisticated fig leaves that cover deep inadequacy that lies in all fallen men irrespective of culture. This means that in terms of relationships and dependence, men and women experience them differently.

If boys need to separate from the mother in order to connect with their masculinity, women do not need to separate from the mother to feel feminine, and so early on masculinity becomes basically defined by separation and femininity becomes defined by attachment. Could this

---

[15] C S Lewis, *Perelandra* (London: Pan Books, 1943) p.125

explain why men feel threatened by intimacy while longing for it at the same time, thus they can be characterised by an unconscious ambivalence without even realising it? If men are threatened by relationships because they need to find their masculinity in separation, women feel threatened by separation and maybe don't see themselves as individuals in the same way men do.

Gordon Dalbey, a speaker and author who also tackles the complex subject of damaged masculinity states that

> *'Here, then, is the cr ux of the matter. For life in the church of Jesus Christ focuses entirely upon 'relationships', and particularly issues of 'dependency'- relationships with God and with one another, and dependency upon God and with one another. If for males the thr ust of maturing to manhood is in the direction of 'separation and individuation', then clearly the church and males are moving in opposite directions from the ver y outset, and the issue of conversion to a Christian life-orientation is far more complex and demanding for men than for women'* [16]

This is where we men have to come out of our caves of independence as we alienate ourselves from the very healing and self-worth we need. Since God has designed us to function most healthily only in relationship to Him and to one another, sooner or later the need for relationship will surface within the souls of men. As isolated men not ready to 'unzip our guts' to be transparent and vulnerable to develop real relationships, we tend to control what we most fear. The man who fears relationships will therefore try to control his relationship with God and with others.

---

[16] Gordon Dalbey, *Healing the Masculine Soul* (W Publishing Group, 2003) p.207

Men usually do this through systems of law and institutional hierarchies, which tragically reduce relationship to something manageable. So institutional Christianity along with the effects of secularism do not necessarily facilitate men to connect with their core masculinity and to express it, and thus men who control, however subtle and ostensibly 'spiritual' it may appear, will only have the opposite effect of driving men away to continue their search to live from their masculine core. Moreover, institutional Christianity based on control, will fail to see how necessary it is for boys, young men and broken immature men to experience initiation rites of passage into a more authentic masculinity.

Initiation in Scripture

Men in Scripture manifested their wounded-ness in different ways but also their lives were marked by initiation rites of passage. Moses began life with no father and as a young man depended on his privileged position in Egypt as well as his physical strength to achieve his ambitions, so his status and strength defined his manhood in a way, a bit like some men in contemporary western culture. However, after committing murder, he was a wanted man and it was only after forty long years of being humbled in the wilderness that he became the humble but courageous leader and man God wanted him to be.

Moses' privileged position, his physical strength and status relate to the material success that we in the West are conditioned to believe is the sum total of our life and being. In other words the so called 'good life' of wife, children, nuclear family, nice job with good income, nice house in the suburbs, nice comfortable church… and we've arrived. Being part of a huge fortress, whether it's a corporation, institutional church, or government/economic empire has nothing to do with the desert. In fact these scenarios are an antidote to life in the desert.

If you have money, status, recognition, some prestige and reputation, healthy kids with good morals, or whatever makes you feel 'successful', means you don't ever have to actually *feel* anything. Our culture is so fragmented and shallow, that we have no real hope in anything substantial. The desert is where you learn and suffer, it's where we are broken by God, and the walls of our self-protection and of the false self are dismantled.

Moses may have been a big shot in the Palace of Pharaoh as we all can feel successful in our own ways, but in the desert it hits you hard and it has to, because the warrior in us needs to be wounded to become more balanced and integrated and to get perspective on our humanity, our fragility. In the desert you come face to face with yourself; you discover how weak and how wicked you really are. You get to see and feel deeply, your own fears, sickness, addictions, lust, pleasures and you face your own limitations, your own lies and self-delusion, your own humanity.

You face wild beasts, deep dark places within yourself which scare you, desperation like you have never known. You are totally and utterly alone in the desert; you feel homeless and like an empty rootless refugee who does not belong anywhere or to anything or any place. In the desert there is a cave and you sometimes want to die because it feels like death. But all true spiritual life comes out of death and this is where our real authentic power lies as men, through spending time in the desert.

God breaks you, strips you to the core in the desert and you lie there beaten to the ground knowing somewhere deep inside that you will never be the same again. Part of you is dead; it is a kind of baptism. Welcome to the desert. I spent many years in my own desert; became permanently and painfully disabled, have many physical scars and encounters with death. God took me there to initiate me and deal with me. I will talk about this in chapter five.

Jacob was also as a young boy alienated from his father who showed favouritism to the elder brother Esau, but also because of his mother's controlling influence. He did not really begin the journey toward true masculinity until after he had left home, separate from his strong mother and fend for himself. After twenty years of hard labour and discipline he finally became the man God intended when he wrestled with God and his name was changed to Israel. God had touched Jacob to the bone, at the very core of his identity. 'What's your name' God asked which means 'Who are you'.

Jacob which means 'the one who grabs from behind, 'the cheater', the one who will do anything to keep someone else from getting ahead of him, thus represents our fallen nature. He wrestles with God in the dark and alone, just like we will all need to do at some point for this is God initiating us into manhood. He becomes 'Israel' meaning 'prince with God', or 'the struggler with God'.

The story of Jacob tells us that before you can love somebody else, or be loved by someone else, you have to wrestle with that part of yourself that gets scared when love starts breaking down your defences. Men especially need this wrestling match with God in order to be the fully engaged leaders they are called to be. Men with a 'limp' whether literal or metaphorical have the capacity to be real so that others are free to also be real.

True power comes from having spent a season in the desert, encountering the enemy, learning to wield the sword of truth and returning in the power of the Spirit. So the message and actually good news is that what men need comes only in the terrifying, painful initiation of the Cross, where we die to our proud natural selves and rise anew in resurrection power as beloved sons of Father God. The Good News therefore is to feel God's grip on your flesh, and to cry out your name for who you are without him and to feel this brokenness even down to the bone, to receive the blessing of a new person, a new name as you finally let go, cling to God and at last to follow.

Joseph was also separated from his father at a young age, partly through his own youthful immaturity of boasting that he was somehow more special than his brothers, plus his father did not help by giving him a coat of many colours. It was only through many years of suffering and hardship that he reached his true stature as the man God called him to be. Psalm 105v18 implies that the iron around Joseph's neck 'came into his soul' so that he became a man of iron.

It was the sufferings of these men that basically initiated them into a much deeper more abiding sense of true manhood that was able to sacrificially fight for others, but it involved a separation from their present life, a transition into a new way of being, and incorporation into a transformed character able to lead others. Furthermore, these men did not have strong healthy masculine input from their fathers, so God himself can initiate us into manhood.

Appearance, occupation, competence, money, wealth, possessions, success, status, physical strength, family, sex, sport, control, are some of the familiar ways men define themselves and even these methods can change. In the 60s and 70s the more effeminate, gentle understanding image was 'in' but in the 80s it was the tough competitive image, and now in a multi-cultural pluralistic society men seem confused about what makes them distinctive and what defines true masculinity. For example in today's society, the term metro-sexual is like a merging of both male and female which is more androgynous than overtly male, but for all the searching for a model of manhood, there has not really been a universal model for true manhood, or has there?

What is authentic masculinity?

Attempting to write about masculinity and initiation and what it is to be a man are themes of much of world literature, particularly heroic literature. For it is concerned in a special way with the masculine, because masculine development is manifest in a dramatic way in the literary figure of the hero, a model for men in his culture, including the initiations that a male must go through to become a man. The hero leaves normal life to confront death and returns to ordinary life to assume social responsibilities.

The first Adam lost the blueprint that God gave him in Genesis chapter two but could this mean that the Last Adam can help us gain a true understanding of masculinity? Simply being an adult male is not enough; one must in addition be a man, which means more than simply having a male body. Being a man in the fullest sense is a matter of the will, a choice to live in a certain way. Jesus' life is that of the hero and is therefore the consummation of masculinity.

Jesus was initiated into manhood from age 12 when we can see that he separated from his mother; for Jewish boys were accepted into a man's world when they reached twelve years of age and Luke specifically states this fact (Luke 2v42) So separation from his mother and coming into manhood was celebrated when he went up to the Temple for the Feast of the Passover.

From this moment though, he demonstrated an awareness of emotional separation from his parents and he now began to define himself by his relationship with his heavenly Father. His parents left Jerusalem, but Jesus stayed behind in the Temple without their knowledge it would seem. When they eventually found him, his mother rebuked him, but Jesus took his initiation into manhood seriously and seemed to presume that his parents had done the same 'Why is it that you sought me, did you not know that I must be about My Father's business'? (Luke 2v49).

To the modern western mind-set this reply of Jesus will probably seem bewildering, for how can Jesus be a model for us when he speaks to his mother in a somewhat disrespectful manner? Any confusion or difficulty in this incident between Jesus and his mother implies that we still do not understand that separation from the mother and initiation into manhood are essential. However, Western culture does not provide any acceptable model of separation and initiation which is recognised by all parties concerned and this is compounded by a western phenomenon of single parent families where the majority are mothers.

This is not to blame single parents, but young boys are not being initiated into manhood, so countless numbers of men stay as 'adolescents' and struggle deeply with being stuck in a place of anger, addiction and with commitment to women and living sacrificially for them. This incident then in the Temple during the early life of Jesus highlights the important milestone of separation from the mother and initiation into manhood by other men. We see again later in Jesus' life that Mary tried to pressure him at the wedding in Cana (John 2v4). His resistance of her is drawing a line in the sand by stating his life was no longer under her control and that he was fully committed to his Father's will.

Taking up and wielding the sword of truth

Jesus separated from his mother then and was then initiated into the world of men because this was normal for his culture. As an adult at his baptism he received the affirmation and love from his Father 'You are My Beloved Son, In You I am well pleased' (Luke 3v22) so his true identity is deeply embedded in him. When a man or woman becomes a follower of Jesus, they are also enlisted into warfare, for there is an enemy, and Jesus was tempted in all ways just as we are.

Following his baptism therefore, Satan attacked Jesus in the areas of his identity 'if you are the Son of God command this stone to become bread' (v3). In other words 'use your power to satisfy your own fleshly desires'. Then the enemy suggested that Jesus test the Father's love for him by throwing himself off the highest pinnacle of the Temple to see if God would send his angels to save him (v5-60 Finally, he offered Jesus a short cut to fame and success 'all this I will give you if you bow down and worship me'.

Every time he was tempted Jesus wielded the sword of truth against the enemy. This implies that true masculinity belongs to men who survive the hardships of the wilderness and become warriors; men who recognise and discern the enemy's strategies and defeat him by wielding the sword of truth. Other traits that Jesus had as a model for true masculinity were leadership and authority but without coercion or manipulation. He had self-discipline and courage, so time spent in the Father's presence gave him the energy and courage to persevere.

Like Jesus, we are in the world but not of it, and only courageous and self-disciplined men and women can keep those two worlds in their correct perspective and maintain composure and poise. The fact that Jesus wept at Lazurus' tomb, and wept over Jerusalem and was frequently moved with compassion, means that he was a man who was also able to manifest a full range of emotions, he was not afraid to show his true feelings.

He was also totally dependent on the Father and his relationship with the Father was more important than life itself (John 4v34). This life of dependence on the Father is the opposite of what most men in Western culture view as masculinity, namely to be very independent, so according to the world's way of thinking, a strong man is independent, the master of his own destiny, the captain of his own ship so he is very much in control (or so he thinks). Conversely, Jesus was totally dependent and had deep intimate communion with the Father, he was fierce in wielding the sword of truth against the enemy and was both Lamb and Lion, so he balanced both feminine and masculine within his being.

If then our true authentic masculine hearts that willingly sacrifice and offer life giving energy, are buried, we need something to open our hearts in order to journey into them so as to find them again and live from our uniqueness. For so many men become hypnotised by consumerism and the numbing effects of overstimulation of the mass media.

Consequently men are 'taken out' by becoming so comfortable, numb, domesticated, complacent, docile, passive, indifferent, and settle for the status quo in our anaesthetised private little bubbles. There are battles to fight and men are missing in action, like I was for so many years. Can the dry bones of buried masculinity live? Yes because the man was created first and God is not going to give up and abandon the male's leadership responsibility just for the sake of changing cultural attitudes.

The Fatherlessness of the Twentieth Century

So we are still following the waters that are continuing to trickle further down the mountain into mainstream society. Secularism leaves man totally alone in the universe, western culture has no clear initiation rites of passage, and so the main historical and social changes and upheavals across the 20th and into the 21st century can be characterised by an epidemic of Fatherlessness or Father Absence. Mary Pytches points out that

> 'During the First World War in particular, the casualties were enormous: A whole generation of men was lost, and future generations were blighted as a result. Nine million people were killed and seventeen million were wounded, of whom a third became invalids. Four million women were

widowed, twice as many children were orphaned' [17].

When you add to this the effects of World War Two with an estimated 50 million casualties, the Great Depression where 14 million men in America were unemployed as a result of the Wall Street crash in 1929 and 2 million unemployed in Britain, two World Wars and this Great Depression of economic recession severely crushed the men of America and Europe. Countless thousands of children were left fatherless. Another effect was that women had to step into men's shoes and do men's jobs. Thus the springboard for the next wave of feminism after the suffragettes was birthed.

After the end of World War Two most of the territories under British rule were given independence and so the British Empire was at an end, and from 1948 West Indians and Asians in the 60s and 70s began to emigrate to the UK and America. The Western world was now becoming multicultural and pluralistic, so masculinity was no longer dominated by a Caucasian patriotic nationalist male identity rooted in the colonial enterprise. It was no longer mono-cultural. In this sense the colonial enterprise actually caused contemporary multi-culturalism and its fruits of religious and secular pluralism and eventually a philosophical relativism that was the polar opposite of the mono-culture of colonialism.

From 1964-70 there was a liberalisation of laws in homosexuality, contraception, abortion and divorce to apparently 'transform Britain into a more tolerant and civilised society' under Harold Wilson's Labour Government. Contraception meant that marriage began to decline in importance and couples could now live together in co- habitation as long as it suited them, without risk of having children. Divorce and breakdown of marriage and

---

[17] Mary Pytches, *A Fathers Place* (New Wine Publishers, 1993 Chronicle of the World London: Longman/Chronicle communications p.1072)

thus single parent families began to emerge during this period.

Martin Holborn and Mike Haralambos in their extensive volume of Sociology, Themes and Perspectives state that

> *'The Divorce Reform Act, which came into force in 1971, no longer emphasised the idea of matrimonial offence and so avoided the need for 'guilty par ties'. It defined the grounds for divorce as 'the irretrievable breakdown of the marriage'. This made divorce considerably easier and accounts in par t for the dramatic rise in the number of divorces in 1971'* [18]

Furthermore, they conclude their section on marriage and divorce that a decline in the rate of marriage, increasing co- habitation, rising numbers of single parent families and single person homes and the increase in marital breakdown all seem to suggest the decline of marriage as an institution in modern Britain. Through the introduction of the Pill women had more control over their bodies and of their fertility and so the changing status of women and the personal preferences of individuals began to challenge and change family life and with it the roles and definition of manhood.

Something called unisex came in during this time and gender roles including gender distinctions became blurred. Men began to 'get in touch with their feminine side' and militant feminists expressed more masculine traits. So from the 1960s onward the pressure on society to change was of colossal proportions. During this so called 'cultural revolution' of the sixties the worldview changed even more.

The Civil Rights movement however necessary and essential for Black people, in retrospect has been unwittingly

---

[18] Martin Holborn and Mike Haralambos (Sociology, Themes and Perspectives, (Harper Collins Publishers, 2004) p.523

a catalyst for the demand for Human Rights for numerous minority groups since then. Politics became and still is like a new tribalism pandering to the demand for Rights of specialist interest groups. Women were at the forefront of the demand for Equal Rights and so the 'gender war' has been almost totally focused on Equal Rights.

This demand for Rights has almost totally ignored the essential fact of gender distinctions, so Western culture has not really worked out gender distinctions due to deconstruction of previous norms. Both men and women have caused gender confusion not just because they could not work out who would do what in the home, but more fundamentally gender distinctions are rooted in creation. So has the disregard of gender distinction left Western culture lost in confusion? Does that mean that the Church has nothing to say to the contemporary generation in the 21st century?

John Piper states

> 'He has shown us in Scripture the beauty of manhood and womanhood in complementary harmony. He has shown us the distortions and even horrors that sin has made of fallen manhood and womanhood. Our knowledge is not perfect. But we are not so adrift as to have nothing to say to our generation about the meaning of manhood and womanhood and its implications for our relationships…
> In the Bible, differentiated roles for men and women are never traced back to the fall of man and woman into sin. Rather, the foundation of this differentiation is traced back to the way things were in Eden before sin warped our relationships. Differentiated

roles were corrupted, not created by the fall.
They were created by God'. [19]

The worldview of the sixties was one of Hedonism and about freedom without restraint while deconstructing previous traditional cultural norms and values. Western culture in the 1960s changed radically into a Babylonian neo-Pagan society where new forms of spirituality became very popular like the New Age movement that teaches we can become 'God'. The original meaning of Babel in Genesis 11 means 'confusion' and neo-Pagan simply means a new form of Paganism which worships the earth and rejects the Creator.

As I have specified Secularism became the dominant overarching worldview about reality within a closed system where all is physical and only physical. Because humans have been created in the image of the Triune God, we cannot live in a vacuum, we are created to worship, and as Romans chapter

1 teaches us, fallen man takes from something within the creation and worships the creature rather than the creator (Romans 1v 18-32). In verse 25 the Apostle Paul states that they 'exchanged the truth of God for a lie'. This is what Western culture did in the 60s en masse, it exchanged the truth of God in every way, and in particular it deconstructed God's revelation in His Word about gender distinctions. The waters are still trickling downwards.

James Dobson in his book *Bringing up Boys* addresses the effects of certain forces in the late sixties that took the world by storm. He states

> *'They are the sexual revolution and radical feminism, which have contributed mightily to masculine confusion today. That was a period*

---

[19] John Piper and Wayne Grudem, *Recovering Biblical Manhood and Womanhood*, (Crossway Books, 1991) p.35

*when Western nations seemed to wobble on
the brink of insanity. Time called it 'a knife
edge that severed past from the future'.
This era brought a new way of thinking and
behaving that is still with us today. Never has a
civilisation so quickly jettisoned its dominant
value system, yet that is what occurred within
a single decade. Not only did traditional moral
standards and beliefs begin to crumble, but
the ancient code governing how men and
women related to each other was turned
upside down. It precipitated a war between
the sexes that is still being waged these many
years later. History teaches that the young
and vulnerable suffer most from the ravages
of war'.* [20]

One of the characteristics of Paganism is that it is deeply feminist. The issue for women was one of equality and the natural solidarity of women gave these issues of Equal Rights inspiration that was powerful. By the 1970s and 80s a militant feminist movement had grown out of the women's movement and this radical feminism attacked marriage and family life. Men were not needed as providers, or protectors, nor even as pro-creators. Marriage and family life have been viewed by extreme feminists as blockage to their 'freedom', independence and equality. Mary Pytches writes

*'Although a man is still needed for his sperm,
the feminist would deny him the right to be
the father his child needs fearing that his
par ticipation would become a means to
exer t control and dominance... after years
of deliberation, the law courts upheld the*

---

[20] James Dobson, *Bringing Up Boys* (Tyndale House Publishers, 2001) p.161

*feminist demands to undermine the rights of
the father regarding the unborn child. In 1981
the European Court of Justice confirmed
that the father has no right to be consulted
respecting the termination of pregnancy'* [21]

This trend has led to men being referred to as 'Sperm
Donors'. Women's initial cause was legitimate because they
needed to find their place in the world after the Second World
War, but it spiralled into guerrilla warfare and distorted its
original intent by attacking the very identity and purpose
of men.

The problem was that masculinity had traditionally been
defined in the roles of *provider, protector* and procreator. If
these roles have been in place for hundreds if not thousands
of years and are suddenly set aside in such a short space
of time, then how do men now define themselves as men?
If there is such a concept and reality as a male identity
crisis, then it is not inseparable from the huge changes
in the worldview and these previous explicit male roles
disappearing so quickly.

Furthermore, the changes from manufacturing
industries where men worked in an all-male environment
and created, invented, made and produced things to the
mixed gender environment of service industries which
is technology based is not a peripheral point – for this
cultural shift in industry is about the upheaval of entire
communities. Also the camaraderie that men experienced
within manufacturing industries is gone with everything
that entails. The disappearance then of traditional roles that
defined men as provider, protector, and procreator set aside
relatively quickly and combined with these historical and
social changes resulted in a huge Father absence in society
that is of epidemic proportions.

---

[21] Mary Pytches, *A Fathers Place* (New Wine Publishers, 1993) p.22

These cultural changes combined with major decline of men from the Church are also inseparable from the silent epidemic of fatherlessness. If it was a physical disease it would be labelled an epidemic but it is invisible and yet the effects of fatherlessness could not be more overt, up close and personal. The point is that the roles and relationships of men and women have completely changed *in the last few decades*. Men began to wonder what made them distinctive. This setting aside of traditional roles of provider, protector and procreator feels very confusing, frightening and even dangerous to many men. The goalposts have not only moved, they have emigrated and so the waters have trickled so far downwards that men have nothing left to define their manhood by.

So where do I fit into these huge changes across the twentieth century and how has this affected me as a man? For most of my life I have not had a clue about what is distinctive about being a man. Having grown up in a large foster home and not really experiencing the love of a mother and father, my life has been up to this point marked by a repetitive rootlessness. I did not have an idea of what I was good at or what I wanted to do with my life until my late thirties, early forties when I re-educated myself and became a teacher of Further Education after a long journey of recovering from a car accident that left me with a permanent and painful disability.

Therefore, in terms of having the presence that comes from a deep abiding sense of manhood that initiates and offers healthy masculine strength to a woman, I simply did not have any of that. I drifted aimlessly for many years not feeling like I belonged anywhere. Terms like provide, protect, lead, initiate have been alien to me. This is why strong masculine presence is crucial to initiate boys into authentic manhood. I did not have it so I entered adult life without a map so to speak. Deep inside I was a lost, insecure little boy roaming alone the jungle of the world, like a lion cub cut off from its parents fending for itself and unsure of it's true identity. However, my deepest wound was that of an orphan spirit as noted above, and in a fatherless society it is so utterly common yet so tragically ignored by both the culture and the Church.

I was illegitimate when I was born; both my mother and father were from Trinidad & Tobago, the southernmost Caribbean Island. So I grew up in England as a result of the collapse of the British Empire and subsequently it became a culture of pluralism with a melting pot of cultures and beliefs, and eventually this produced relativism, which is where we are today. This is how I came to be born in the UK, the end of an empire and the bringing in of West Indians and Asians from 1948 to the early 1970s. So I was born into a culture that was about to fragment and have its very foundation slowly eroded.

The Fatherlessness that resulted from two world wars and the Great Depression was now escalating at greater speed.

No strong healthy masculine presence or role models, no initiation into manhood, so a life of rootless wandering on the fringes not knowing who I was or what I had to offer. This was me, but a life changing seismic shift in my heart and my manhood healed my deepest wounds, this totally radical transforming ferocious covenant unconditional crazy love unchained my heart and set me free. This shift is called The Fathers Embrace and every man, woman and child needs it because we have been created for God and God is love and with all his heart he longs to embrace us and kiss us and father us in the orphan areas in our hearts. We all have these to a lesser or greater degree because we have all had imperfect blueprints of fatherhood. In short, we all need to become The Beloved sons and daughters of Abba Father Two of the main ways this damages us is in relationship with women and our working life. If we have not been taught about how to pursue a woman and what is happening to us through our teenage years, we learn it from our peers and boys cannot initiate boys into manhood, nor can mothers. In short, we struggle deeply in our relationship with women because if we have not been affirmed and loved for who we are rather than what we do, we tend to feel a hesitancy, an uncertainty about how to offer a woman authentic strength that allows her femininity to flourish.

Also we struggle with what we want to do with our life, we're not sure what our skills and abilities are, so we don't really know who we are. Our peers then become like a surrogate family, but again boys cannot initiate boys and neither can mothers. It takes men who have been initiated into manhood themselves and to bring boys into the community of men. I not only lacked the confidence with women especially in my twenties, but I did not have a clue about what I was good at.

This obviously happens with boys who had a father and mother, but a generational fatherlessness has meant that generations of boys do not get what they really need – strong engaged committed fathers who can teach and bring them into the world of men, so they know their place in the world. However, this is where we can take a step out of our emotional caves, by realising that our fathers could not give us what they did not have. If they themselves did not get the essential stuff of being brought into manhood through initiation rites of passage, this enables us to have compassion on them and to work through heart forgiveness and move on. Men used to know their place in the world, but this is no longer the case, you just have to look around, there are broken addicted men who have been taken out left, right and centre.

Un-fathered men lack confidence in their manhood and often we try to cover a sense of deep shame, inadequacy, anger or sadness in a number of ways. As Adam and Eve tried to cover their nakedness so we also hide behind a variety of 'fig leaves', the list is very long. Because of this 'Adam and

Eve' complex that all men and women inherit irrespective of different cultural norms and values, sometimes we need to take an intentional journey that includes a process of self- discovery.

This means that we need to let go of all the ways we have protected ourselves. Shame and blame sum up the way Adam and Eve reacted as a result of their choice to rebel against God, and resulted in deep alienation. It is a four-fold and profound alienation. As a result of the historic space-time Fall of man, human beings are alienated from the one true living God who is a Triune relational being, alienated from ourselves and our true God designed humanity and gender roles in creational design, alienated from each other as men and women-again as the Creator designed for us, and alienated from the physical world in terms of living as stewards of all creation in mutual submission.

A generational fatherlessness in the culture meant that were not too many examples of elders who could initiate me into my own Christ-like masculinity. I backslid from my Christian faith and integrated into the hippie scene, which was like a substitute family for me, but my way of trying to cover my own wounds through drugs and 'rebelling'. The hippie image was my fig leaf during my twenties. This lasted for about six years but I was so lost, empty, and so unfulfilled and insecure. I needed to get back with my Lord and Saviour Jesus, which eventually meant coming 'home' to the Fathers Embrace. I will go into more detail in chapter five but how is Western culture doing then in relation to father absence?

Contemporary Fatherlessness

In his recent book entitled *'I am Your Father'* Mark Stibbe quotes from a recent study referred to as 'Fatherless America' the conclusion drawn are that Fatherless children in the USA are:

'8 times more likely to go to prison, 5 times more likely to commit suicide, 20 times more likely to have behavioural problems, 20 times more likely to become rapists, 32 times more likely to run away, 10 times more likely to abuse chemical substances, 9 times more likely to drop out of high school, 33 times more likely to be seriously abused, 73 times more likely to be fatally abused, one-tenth as likely to get A's in school, on average have a 44% higher mortality rate, on average have a 72% lower standard of living (For full details of these statistics see http://www.massey.ac.nz/~kbirks/gender/econ/nodad.html)

Mark Stibbe argues, as do many that Britain is now fatherless. He continues

> *'Not long ago a UK prison chaplain decided to offer the 500 male prisoners in his prison the opportunity to say thank you to their mums... the offer was accepted by every single one of the prisoners. The chaplaincy was so encouraged by the response that they started planning for Father's Day. In May they offered the same 500 prisoners the same option – this time a free card to sign and send to their fathers, saying 'thank you'. Not one of the prisoners accepted the offer. Not one card was sent'.* [22]

He goes on to say that this story vividly illustrates the point that no one can now run away from, namely that Fatherlessness is now rampant in British culture that goes

---

[22] Mark Stibbe, *I Am Your Father* (Monarch Books, 2010) p.22-3 (Prison statistics from a speech by Iain Duncan Smith at the Prison Ministry Conference on 20 November 2009 at Holy Trinity Brompton, South Kensington. The UNICEF statistic is from *'Child Poverty in Perspective: An overview of child wellbeing in rich countries'*, Innocenti Report Card 7, 2007, UNICEF Innocenti Research Centre, Florence, p.4.

back at least a century, certainly since the time of the First World War. He pinpoints the root problem when he states

> *'there has been a demonic assault against fatherhood in the UK and worldwide'.*

Fatherlessness is our most destructive social trend and the answers cannot be found by politicians, philosophers, sociologists or psychologists, it is a spiritual battle. We are in a war but do we live as if we were at war?

Stibbe again say's

> *'Fatherlessness is now reaping a whirlwind of destruction in UK society. We should not be surprised to hear that there has in recent years been a tripling of children murdering children, that 70 per cent of young offenders come from fatherless homes, that in 2008 11,000 children were treated for addiction to dr ugs and alcohol, that the UK has the highest rate of teenage pregnancy in Western Europe, and that it is witnessing an unprecedented surge in street-gang membership in its inner cities. UNICEF's 2007 report on childhood development found that out of all the industrialised nations, Britain is the worst country for a child to grow up in (it came 21st out of 21) – far worse than all the other countries in terms of pover ty, happiness, relationships and risk'* [23]

Do we as the Church live as though we were at war? It would change our perspective both individually and

---

[23] Mark Stibbe, *I Am Your Father* (Monarch Books, 2010) p.24

corporately. We have travelled from the Industrial Revolution up to the 21st century and like the avalanche of snow coming down the mountain in the Swiss mountain village, so fatherlessness has escalated and society is literally breaking apart. It is possible to overemphasise spiritual warfare, the tendency usually is to lean toward one of two extremes, either there are demons everywhere or it is ignored completely, and both of these are dangerous and ironically allow the enemy a foothold without us even knowing it because of lack of discernment.

However, Scripture is very clear that Christians are in a spiritual warfare situation, and we need to cross our own metaphoric Jordan and fight the giants that we face. Fatherlessness – both natural and spiritual is one of the main giants. Where are the Joshua's and Caleb's in local churches who will be spiritual fathers, and mentors, who will spend time with boys, young men and broken men like Jesus did, to minister healing, counsel, do warfare, train, invest and release? Busyness today feels like the Philistine hordes like the sand on the seashore, but are we prepared to fight the giant of Busyness together, get real with each other and fight for each other in the trenches *together?*

There is a lot of pain out there and some of the symptoms of an orphan heart in us such as abandonment, rejection, loneliness, hopelessness, worthlessness, sadness, insecurity, hyper-sensitivity, fear and poverty are all things that I myself have lived with most of my life, but there is healing for this emotional pain and it can only come from walking through the process where we experientially become the Beloved of God, through communion with him, authentic community and then out of our healing we can find our calling and minister to others.

Spiritual fathers and mentors needed.

Only male elders who have had enough of their self-life crucified to fight the enemy through a journey of brokenness and are able to be vulnerable with other men can initiate boys. If the hearts of fathers are not restored to their children, both naturally and spiritually, Malachi 4v6 states that the Lord will 'strike the earth with a curse'. When relationships between the generations are estranged, they are quite literally cursed.

Trust needs to be rebuilt, for it is so broken down in contemporary society, one of the reasons being because some parents have neglected their children at the expense of their own happiness and agendas. Healthy strong fathers bring strength; they form identity, stability and balance to a family. A natural father is meant to be a protector, a provider, a source of guidance and discipline for his children, so that clear boundaries are formed and children can grow up to make choices that are shaped by these healthy boundaries.

Spiritual fatherlessness is such a weakness in the Body of Christ today; pastors can be so busy it is difficult to develop a genuine relationship with them. So a huge vacuum has been created through the scarcity of mature godly fathering and mentoring. Father's in the Lord are so desperately needed and this does not have to be pastors or leaders. Authority does not come from a position or a right, or a name on the door, it is the outworking of who you are, your character, and especially the anointing of God's Spirit, it is the sum total of a person's character, gifts, wisdom, maturity and servant heart attitude.

Moreover, a leader cannot force a person to agree with him/her, otherwise anything above and beyond the freedom to choose leads to manipulation or even coercion. Fathers in the Lord understand these principles because they know the character of the Father, so they are able to relax in their ministry to others, although that does not mean that they are not firm at times or cannot confront when necessary. The difference is that they do that because the Father would have them to do it, and not because they are a leader or because of their position.

Jesus is the model for us to follow. As Floyd McClung says in *The Father Heart of God*

> *'Jesus fathered his disciples in four stages: He did it and they watched, He did it and they helped, They did it and He helped, They did it and He left. Being a good father, whether in the church or the home, has more to do with the atmosphere we create than the words we speak. People will remember our attitude and actions, how we say things, far longer than the actual words we speak. Those attitudes, and our underlying philosophy of life and ministry, create an atmosphere everywhere we go. We bring it with us'* [24]

The love of the Father transforms us.

However, only those who are totally convinced and who have also experienced the Fathers love and know him intuitively and whose hearts are deeply rooted and grounded in his love can freely and lovingly pass on a healthy spiritual inheritance to the next generation or even their peers. Everyone needs to be exposed to the extravagant healing love of Jesus for it is this that sets the heart free to live courageously and in a radically new way.

The Apostle John had previously been hungry for status and power. He had some rough edges. John and his brother James were nicknamed the 'sons of thunder' (Mark 3v17)

---

[24] Floyd McClung, *The Father Heart of God*, (Kingsway Communications Limited, 2001) p.122-3

and they asked Jesus if they could order fire to come down from heaven to destroy a Samaritan village because they refused to allow Jesus and the disciples to pass through. James and John also made the other disciples angry when they asked if they could sit on Jesus' right and left hand in glory (Mark 10v35-45) and even sent their mother to ask Jesus this same favour (Matthew 20v20-21) showing all the signs of insecurity and self- seeking pride.

However, as John spent more time with Jesus, he was changed. Long and lengthy exposure to the extravagant ferocious love of Jesus transformed the 'Son of thunder' to 'the disciple who Jesus loved' (John 19v26; 20v2; 21v7, 20). Can we be the one who also leans on the Lord's bosom? Are we also able to say of ourselves 'I am the one who Jesus loves'? We can, because John also recorded the secret of his love for them...'As the Father has loved me, so I have loved you' (John 15v9). How amazing is that? John received a revelation that Jesus loved him in the same way and manner that the Father loved the Son.

This revelation of the Father's love opened his heart and transformed him so that he could give love freely to the next generation. Later we see that John prayed and imparted the Holy Spirit to Philip's converts in Samaria, the very people on whom he had wanted to call down fire for refusing to hear the gospel (Acts 8v14-16). What is even more incredible is that we are also loved by the Father in the very same way, for he loves us in the same way that he loves Jesus!. I hasten to add though, that we need to hold a delicate balance between pointing people to the Father, and mentoring them to grow spiritually.

For those who aspire to be spiritual fathers then, we need to have had our insecurities dealt with, the ways that we hide behind our fig leaves to cover our deep inadequacy as men, and becoming beloved sons of the Father help to dissolve our rough edges as it did for the one who knew he was the one 'who Jesus loved'. The life that a mentor or spiritual father offers though comes through their own experience of initiation as they are separated from their past, go through the ambiguity of transition, before they incorporate into the new life and calling that crystallises out of their time in the desert. Yet the Church does not initiate.

This can only come from the Father's Embrace through the Word and a power encounter with the Holy Spirit, in whatever way he chooses to touch our spirit with revelation of his love. In short, we need the same as Jesus received at his baptism; we need to hear 'You are my beloved son, in you I am well pleased' and our hearts need to 'be seized with the power of a great affection'.

As the Apostle Paul lamented to the Corinthian Church 'you have ten thousand instructors but you do not have many fathers' (1 Cor 4vl5). Fathers in the faith are meant to deeply and intimately, intuitively and experientially *know* Abba Father. Fathers like this are called to be the foundation of both the Church and indeed the culture. For without a foundation, the storms come and great shall be the crash of that house.

CHAPTER 4

Men are called to be the foundation

God created the man first. Genesis 1v26-28 is the blueprint but in chapter two God gives us more detailed information about the manner in which He made the male and female. The New Testament confirms this 'For it was Adam who was first created, and then Eve' (1Timothy 2v13). First He *formed* the man and this speaks of the intimacy of a Potter making and shaping something from the dust of the ground. He then breathed into his nostrils the breath of life and the man became a living soul (2v7)

How close do you have to be to breathe into someone's nostrils? The man was made first then and there was a break in time before he created the woman. What we can learn about God's purposes for the man by what he saw, heard and learnt during this interlude of time is of the utmost importance because it shows us the crucial components of the man's priority, his purpose and also the assignment that God gave to the man. The man's *priority* is to be the foundation.

Only the male came directly from the earth so he was designed by God to be the *foundation* of the human family. The woman came out of the man because she was designed to rest on the man-to have the male as her support. God did not begin earthly society with a family; he began it with one man. God planned everything before He began to create, he did not make it up as he went along. So He started by laying the foundation and this is the priority in building, you have to start with a strong foundation.

The order in which the man was created then gives us the first indication of his reason for being. Jesus himself spoke of a foundation. He said some build on a foundation of sand and some build on rock. In other words, if the foundation is not right, when a storm hits, the house will crash and fall, whereas the house built on the rock will stand. As we become doers of His Word we ourselves become a strong foundation. Paul also spoke about a foundation 'No one can lay any (spiritual) foundation other than the one already laid, which is Jesus Christ (1 Corinthians 3v11).

Society is only as good as it's men

So as God begins to build the human race he began by placing the man at the bottom of the entire building of humanity. The huge implication for this is that any society is only as good as its men, therefore if men do not learn what it means to be a strong foundation in God, then that society will crash and fall, simple as that. As the above stats show, out of five hundred male prisoners, not one of them made a card to send to their father on Father's Day, and this is only one example of how deep the father wound is.

What does that say about the state of fatherhood? There are second and third generations of single parents now in Western nations, especially Britain and the USA. What about divorce? How do single mothers and children of divorce cope without a foundation? Societies are falling apart because the effects of generational fatherlessness have resulted in men becoming a foundation of sand; they have lost their fundamental purpose, their identity and priority as men.

The strength of any foundation is always measured by how much weight it can bear, so it has to have the first priority because everything else is built on it. A woman, a child, a family needs to be able to lean on a man and know that he is not going to crack. Another thing about a foundation is that it is hidden, you can't see it. We walk on the foundation of our houses all the time which means that it is solid and dependable. Men need to live like the foundation we were created to be and this comes from being rooted in the Word of God so that we can teach others.

Boys, who are not shown how to be a foundation, will not know how to be and do this later in adult life, because they will go through life without a map just like I did for so many years. One way to make decisions is to decide which is important and which is essential and to do the latter. A foundation is essential; men are called to be that foundation.

A vision for manhood

What is essential right now is for the Church to develop a vision of manhood rooted in God's Word. It must also include initiation rites of passage again for boys and youth to bring them into the community of men and support them in the difficult transition into manhood because debatably fatherlessness is the most destructive social trend. Rites of passage can and *must* become part of social policy in communities to arrest the historic fatherlessness and the Church needs to invest in men and be intentional about discipling men to be leaders, mentors, and spiritual fathers. If 93% of families follow the father to Christ according to the Focus on the Family research, this speaks for itself.

Men are called by God to be kings and priests who reign over their sphere of influence, and intercede, have vision and are able to provide for their families and communities. Men are called to be warriors who fight and resist the lies of the evil one who tries to make God as the enemy by getting us to make agreements with his lies about the character of God and projecting a distorted perception of God's character, especially his Father heart. Men are called to be mentors to teach others, men who models, explains, trains, disciples.

Stu Weber who has been a leader of men behind enemy lines in Vietnam as a member of the Special Forces in his book *Tender Warrior* a book about God's intention for men argues that

> *'Four Might Ones are in ever y man; a perfect unity cannot exist but from the universal brotherhood of Eden, the universal man... William Blake, 'The Four Zoas'.*

Stu Weber changes these terms into four pillars of King, Warrior, Mentor and Friend and says that these four pillars can be seen both in the Word of God and in the secular history of man (the four archetypes of King, Warrior, Magician, Lover). The four archetypes in pagan/secular history though, lack the truth that real power comes out of the Cross, where our ideas of manhood are crucified, broken, but resurrected through faith and repentance. The Bible is explicitly and implicitly filled with references to all four pillars. In most men, these pillars are imbalanced, and sometimes abusive, but in the Man who was God-Jesus Christ, they were majestically integrated and balanced. He continues in *Tender Warrior*

> *'The heart of a king is a pro-visionary heart, that looks ahead, watches over, and provides order, mercy and justice. The heart of the warrior is a protective heart, the warrior shields, defends, stands between, and guards. A warrior is a protector. Men stand tallest when they are protecting and defending. The hear t of a mentor is a teaching hear t. The mentor knows.*
>
> *He wants others to know. He models, explains, and trains. He disciples-first his wife and kids, then others. He has a spiritual*

heart...he exercises the energy of initiation and transformation.

The hear t of the friend is a loving hear t. It is a care-giving hear t. Passionate, yes. But more. Compassionate ('I will be with you'). The friend in a man is a commitment maker. And a promise keeper. His is the 'energy that connects men to others and to the world'. Sourced in Scripture, obser ved in histor y, and experienced personally, these four pillars bear the weight of authentic masculinity. They co-exist. They overlap. And when they come together in a man, you will know it. You will feel it. You will be touched by it. Like four strands of steel in a cable, they will hold you'. [25]

As he says the four are inseparable in a good man, and in balance they are every man's purpose, every woman's dream and every child's hope, but abused they are the curse of every man, woman and child. The word passion is rooted and linked to suffering, hence the 'passion of Christ'. Friendship born out of suffering goes deep, develops camaraderie, and God calls us to encourage each other daily (Hebrews 3v13) lest our hearts become hardened. These four words king, warrior, mentor and friend come together and balance in a man's heart that enables a man to be a foundation. In short, the overarching factor and word that defines authentic manhood is the word *Initiation*.

---

[25] Stu Weber, *Tender Warrior* (Multnomah Books, 1993) p.42-3

Again, Stu Weber in Tender Warrior states

> 'The ancient Hebrew word for man is Ish,
> 'piercer'. The term for woman is 'Isha'
> 'pierced one'. While the anatomical or
> sexual elements are clear, the force of the
> words is much larger in scope. The physical
> is a parable of the spiritual. The visible is
> a metaphor for the invisible. The tangible
> speaks for the intangible. At his core a man
> is an initiator – a piercer, one who penetrates
> moves forward, advances toward the horizon,
> leads. At the core of masculinity is initiation-
> the provision of direction, security, stability
> and connection'. [26]

In Psalm 8v5 David asks 'What is man that You are mindful of him' and then he answers 'You have made him a little lower than God, and You have crowned him with glory and honour'. Glory means 'weight' or 'substance'. If these four strands king, warrior, mentor and friend and I would add the calling of priest, then this kind of man will be a strong foundation able to bear the weight of his marriage, his family, to be an agent of change in his Church, in the community, in society, his nation and in the world. Why? Because he leads with a healthy balance of king, warrior, mentor, friend and priest. The man's priority given by God is to not only be the foundation, but God also gave the man certain tasks before he created the woman.

In Genesis 2v15-16 God calls the man to be a *visionary* and *leader.* Eve has not yet been created, so chapter two is focused on God's *calling* for the man and therefore all men.

'Then the LORD God took the man and put him in the Garden of Eden to *tend* and *keep* it. The text continues 'And

---

[26] Stu Weber, *Tender Warrior* (Multnomah Books, 1993) p.45

the LORD God commanded the man saying 'Of every tree of the garden you may freely eat (v17) but of the tree of the knowledge of good and evil you shall not eat, for in the day that you eat of it, you shall surely die'.

The man received all of this information alone, so the man was in charge, responsible, visionary and leader alone who was to guide those who came after him in the ways of God. The man was called to be a visionary and leader before the woman has been created and is responsible for everything under his jurisdiction which as Psalm 115v16 tells us is the whole earth 'but the earth he has given to the children of men'.

This is so crucial for us men to understand because we are not to blame the woman; this is why God went straight to Adam even though Eve was the first one who ate the fruit. Therefore when God asked Adam 'Where are you'(3v9) the question was not in regard to his physical location, God knew that of course. The question 'Where are you'? is a question of position. In other words 'Where are you' in relation to the calling I gave you? You are not fulfilling your position of leadership, what has happened to your wife? The man's purpose was to determine his position and it is the same for men ever since Adam. The man's purpose was not chosen by him, it was designed by the Creator God. If you are a man we are called to be responsible to lead whether we like that or not.

When God gave Adam his command 'do not eat of the tree in the middle of the Garden, the tree of knowledge of good and evil', he said this only to the man before Eve was made yet. So this means it was the man's responsibility to teach and guide her in the Word of God. The man was given the purpose of being the teacher not because he is superior but because he came first, simple as that. This is the pattern that God established and it does not mean women are unable to teach, but that God intended men to be *primarily* responsible for teaching His Ways. The fact that

Eve added to the Word of God in Genesis 3v3 in her reply to the serpent, implies that either Adam failed to teach her the Word of God or she forgot.

God also gave the man the assignment to both tend and keep. *Tend* means to nurture, to cultivate which is where we get our word culture from. The nature of the work that God gave man therefore was to cultivate, to grow and produce to create, invent, explore, and build. A man then is to cultivate people and things, to cultivate everything around him, to make something fruitful and to develop and help to flourish. This came before the Fall so it opens up the question of whether the nature of work is meant to include creativity and cultivation. Now work is also about providing, and *provide* comes from a Latin word meaning 'to see ahead'. So he is to have a vision for his life and he should work to see that it is accomplished for himself, his family, and others.

To *keep* means to protect everything that God had created the Garden, plants, animals and the woman that God was about to create. So a man is made to protect a woman. Everything that is under his care and covering God designed the man to protect. The meaning of Adam from the Hebrew is a generic term for 'mankind'. Why did God choose to *not* name the woman after he created her? Because he wanted the man to be totally responsible for her, and this is why a woman has traditionally taken her husband's name, it is to signify that he is responsible for her. So the overall assignment that God has given to the man and to men in general is to fulfil the role of visionary, leader, teacher, cultivator provider and protector.

For a man to realise his true purpose as the Creator has designed us for, he needs to live out these six roles which basically define a man's fundamental *purpose*. Myles Munroe states in *Understanding the Power and Purpose of Men*

'The male's assignment has revealed six specific purposes that God created the man to fulfil: visionary, leader, teacher, cultivator, provider and protector. If ever y man could live out these six things, he would begin to realise his true purpose as a male....to be a strong man means to discover, understand, and fulfil these basic aspects of purpose... we need to focus on God's purpose, rather than roles'.[27]

So much of the gender confusion in modern life, especially since the sixties, is of over gender *roles*, knowing our fundamental *purpose* rooted in creation then is crucial so as to not assimilate the culture's view of masculinity which tends to blur gender distinctions that is the result of an over emphasis on equality. We are equal but different and we need to know our differences rooted in creation not cultural norms, and of course we have to work out how to apply these six terms that define our purpose as men to whatever culture we live in. Living out these six key words in such a way so as to not perpetuate gender stereotypes is a challenge that is unique to the Church in the particular culture it finds itself in.

Why did God not create or form the woman from the dust of the ground like the man? He used a different method. God formed the man of the dust of the earth (2v7). The Hebrew for 'formed' is *yatsar* meaning to mould as a potter moulds clay, but God 'made' the woman (2v22). The Hebrew word for 'made' is banah which means to 'build or 'construct'. The woman was so much like the man that Adam waxed poetical in saying 'This is now bone of my bones and flesh of my flesh, she shall be called 'woman' because she was taken out of 'man'. There was this beautiful structuring then in the creation of the woman, and because the woman came from

---

[27] Myles Munroe, *Understanding the Power and Purpose of Men* (Whitaker House, 2001) p.89

the man, the man is essentially the giver, the initiator and the woman is essentially the receiver.

God fashioned and constructed the woman to be the receiver and this can be seen in the anatomy of a woman. Her receiving complements the man's giving/initiating. However, in order for the woman to be the receiver the woman has to be different from the man. The man and woman therefore were created, formed, made with complementary designs that reflect their individual roles in the larger purposes for which they were created. The word 'helpmeet' in 2v18 particularly 'meet' actually means 'fit', something that is suitable, compatible or comparable. This means that females are a perfect match for males in fulfilling God's purposes. Men therefore need the help of women in all areas of life not just the family, in all areas of human endeavour.

Male leadership then is intrinsic to the original plan and is not a result of the fall, sin or culture. It is the Creator's original intention. This in no way implies that the man is of more value than the woman, it is a matter of difference of *function* and *role*. Male and female are absolutely of equal value and worth before the Creator God. However, equality does not mean the same or identical. We have different functions just like God the Father, God the Son and God the Holy Spirit do. The Three are absolutely equal but have different functions. It is the same with His image bearers. The Holy Spirit glorifies the person and work of the Son, the Son submits to the Father, so there is mutual submission and harmony in the Godhead. The man is the head of the woman, and Christ is the head of the man.

A husband is called to love his wife even as Christ loved the Church – which means to love sacrificially and to die daily and pick up his cross (Ephesians 5v25, 28) The wife is called to respect the husband (Ephesians 5v33) so it's about love and respect fundamentally. Although a woman will feel that a man needs to earn respect and in a sense he does, but if we understand first and foremost that the man is called to love and the woman to respect, then interaction can flow out of this bedrock foundation that the Lord has instructed.

The man must be prepared to die and bleed first meaning he must lead by living sacrificially. Selfishness and marriage do not make harmonious bedfellows do they? If the man leads by loving sacrificially the woman will find it easier to respect and submit to God's design. Love and Respect clarify and define mutual submission and helps to combat the effects of the fall, so the woman will not desire to rule the man, and the man will not lord it over the woman (Genesis 3v16b). This is something I am learning since I got married a few months ago.

If a man is unable to love sacrificially because of unresolved wounds particularly from his father, then he will feel a deep inadequacy and shame, in short he will feel in his core like an insecure little boy. Men hide this sense of shame at all costs and that is one of our core problems because we have to come out of hiding if we want healing and freedom to live in a new way that gives life and offers depth and courage.

Men very rarely acknowledge this to each other and that is why we need true brothers and fathers to get alongside in our own trenches. Because God has designed the man to lead and love sacrificially, if his own broken, fallen manhood has not been forged out of deep and even desperate dependence on God, then as the man goes, so goes the woman, and the children, the family, the church, the community, the society, the nation, the world.

The enemy knows who we really are, image bearers crowned with glory and honour raised up to be seated in heavenly places in Christ as kings and priests, prophets and warriors and beloved sons of the Father – destined to reign on the new earth with the King of Glory forever. God knows who we really are. All creation knows who we are because it is groaning and waiting for the liberty of the sons of God to be revealed. The problem is we don't seem to know who we really are as men and what we are called to.

Ideas have consequences as I have tried to point out and trace from chapter two and three characterised by an epidemic of Father Absence and Fatherlessness which is debatably the most destructive social trend at this moment in time. However, because the Bible presents a world at war and has been since the very beginning, means that from a biblical perspective history is about what is happening in the spiritual realm. Therefore nothing is going to change deeply and ultimately until we see the attack on fatherhood as a demonic assault across the whole world. Fatherlessness then is a spiritual issue.

Because the backdrop of the biblical worldview is warfare, from Genesis to Revelation, there are 'principalities, powers, rulers of the darkness of this age, spiritual hosts of wickedness in the heavenly places' as the Apostle Paul states in Ephesians chapter 6v12. It is significant therefore that just prior to this he explains God's instructions for children and parents and between husband and wife. Children are to 'honour your father and mother which is the first commandment with promise: 'that it may go well with you and you may live long on the earth'. He then say's in verse 4 of chapter 6 'And you fathers do not *provoke* your children to wrath, but bring them up in the training and admonition of the Lord'.

In other words fathers must not provoke but train, not provoke but instruct, and so enable children to honour them, so if fathers are not training their children, then they are somehow provoking them through neglect. Passivity and masculinity are mutually exclusive, they do not belong together. Men have to be intentionally engaged in their children's lives or the family begins to split in two and society fragments into countless pieces of broken humanity.

This is what has marked the twentieth century. Tragically because of the generational fatherlessness and father absence that is of epidemic proportions, boys are not offered the depth of support and committed masculine engagement that they so desperately need. If boys are not initiated into manhood, what you end up with is a lot of boys in men's bodies particularly in a society that has been progressively feminised. The sins of the fathers are visited to the third and fourth generation, but we can break the cycle...through knowing our fundamental purpose as men, knowing in our hearts we are greatly loved by our majestic King and Abba Father, and being intentional about our calling in our sphere of influence.

The Creation Mandate

Because the term 'man' is a generic phase meaning 'mankind' and the image of God is both male and female (God gives the Creation mandate to '*them*') this means that man and woman are called to steward God's creation as image bearers. The man is the Initiator in all areas of life and the woman is the responder. The creation mandate is crucial for a Christian worldview. Ultimately the biblical worldview is comprehensive enough to explain all of reality and provides us with the big picture on the 'box cover' of a biblical worldview, so that we know where aspects of reality are meant to fit according to the Manufacturers design. As we understand our fundamental task given to us by the Creator God, this will provide the clarity needed to discern the *distinctions* between men and women and consequently that men are called to be the foundation of the Creation mandate with women as helpmeets meaning the same word as is used for God as our helper in times of trouble.

Redemption is not just about being saved *from* sin, it has to be about being saved *to* something and that is to resume the task for which we were originally created. What was the task? It was to be fruitful and multiply, fill the earth and subdue it. There is so much within this simply but profound 'job description'. What the Creator is telling us to do is to explore, invent, create, develop cultures and civilisations and nothing less. This means that men and women are to develop the social world, and subdue the earth meaning to harness the natural world, plant crops, compose music, design computers and everything needed to build cultures and civilisations.

This is what the word 'till' means in Genesis 2v15. The LORD God put the man into the Garden to till and keep it. These words are crucial also for men being the foundation. The meaning of 'till' is to nurture, to care for, to cultivate which is the same root as our word 'culture'. This is one of the main ways we are to express the image of God, by being creative and building cultures then. To 'keep' means to guard, it implies that men will have to fight to preserve all aspects of creation so 'dominion' in Genesis 1v28 ties in with 'till and keep' in 2v15. Dominion does mean to exploit even though as a result of the Fall this is exactly what men have done, exploit nature for their own ends rather than for the Creators glory.

Also the Creation or Cultural Mandate as some prefer, is not exclusively Christian because raising families, creating, exploring, building, developing, making, repairing etc are what all human beings do and so this is telling us what our true nature really is, the things we cannot help doing. This is the way God designed everyone to function and so our purpose is to fulfil our God-given nature.

The Fall did not destroy our original calling, but it made it much more difficult. Our work now from Genesis 3v16-17 is marked by sorrow and hard labour, for the Hebrew uses the same word for the 'labour' of childbearing and the 'labour' of growing food. This suggests that the central tasks of adulthood–raising the next generation and making a living will be fraught with the pain of living in a fallen and broken world. So all our efforts will be twisted and misdirected by sin and selfishness.

The world, our own fallen nature (our flesh) and the devil are the three main enemies we must do battle with in a fallen world, but knowing who we really are as beloved sons and daughters of the Father is crucial to live from approval rather than *for* approval as I have explained at the end of chapter three. This grounding in our beloved-ness as Jesus was at his baptism is the basis for our communion with Abba. Communion with Abba provides our basis for forming authentic community as we love each other with the love of Abba which is comprehensive, sacrificial, giving, friendship, foundational, nurturing, cultivating love.

As He drives us into our own wilderness experiences to test our true identity, and to forge the four pillars of king, warrior, mentor and friend and develops the six aspects of his purpose for us as men – just like our Lord Jesus after his baptism, we come out of our wilderness with a new power. Then we emerge out of the wilderness leaning on the arm of our Beloved, clinging to Him like Jacob whose name was changed to Israel, ready in his timing to be the foundation of our relationships, our marriages, our churches, our communities, society, and our nation and into the world as our mission.

How does this work out practically though? We have responsibilities for our relationship with God, with our wives/partners, for our children, the family, the local church, the community, society, the nation, the world. It starts with us. The challenge is to work toward a biblical balance between all of these key terms to do with the four pillars and the six aspects of our purpose, starting with being committed to God and then our family. It is crucial to work out a balance because too much time spent on any one of the above means that other areas will be neglected.

The blueprint for the building of a nation

At Mount Sinai God begins provides a blueprint for the building of a nation and say's immediately and categorically that the worship of idols is forbidden because He alone has created us and made us for Himself. God then say's that the 'sins of the fathers will be visited onto the children to the third and fourth generation, which is another way of saying that we will reap what we sow. Why is it the sins of the *father's* and not mothers? Because men are called by God to be the foundation of a nation and as already stated as the man goes so goes the woman, the children, the family, the church, the community etc. That's the blueprint; men are called to be the foundation.

When men throughout the world recover their true voice, their true identity, their true calling and destiny, and release their power and recapture the deep fulfilment in following God's call to become authentic men, then the very nature of Christian community will change. We must develop mentors, wise men and women who don't just manage and control and quote Scripture and have lots of programs, but who know how to get to the essence, the core of things, and who have the anointing to release the power of God's supernatural resources to bear on what is really wrong.

The effects on society and the church of having no strong masculine fathers cannot be minimised. Initiation rites of passage are rooted in worldviews and ideas of manhood and when a boy becomes a man. These ideas of initiation rites are about stages of transition, separation from the mother, and initiating into the community of men. They have always been a part of human history and are universally embraced.

The consequences being that a boy is clear about when and how he becomes a man. All cultures need men who can initiate boys into manhood, bring them into the community of men, envision them, disciple, train, mentor and father younger men. As followers of Jesus we have a great and noble calling on our lives and have been brought into a magnificent epic underpinned by warfare. We have been brought into a cosmic battle then, so we need to know how to fight.

From the biblical perspective the whole of reality is spiritual. Paul describes these principalities and powers elsewhere in 2 Corinthians 10v3-5 as '*strongholds*' expressed in 'arguments that exalt themselves against the knowledge of God'. The knowledge of God is revealed in creation, Holy Scripture and the Person of Jesus Christ, in particular his death and resurrection. As a result of the Fall of man in Eden, the mind of man is at enmity with God (Romans 8v7) meaning opposition. The huge historical shift in worldview from a Biblical perspective to a Secular one is an example of the enmity of fallen man in revolt against his Creator. The ideas I have mentioned are actually demonic strongholds from a biblical interpretation of reality.

Men have been 'under a spell', an enchantment, as a result of this onslaught of humanistic worldviews that put man at the centre of things instead of God. This 'spell' is in relation to what God has *called* them to be and we have forgotten *the why* of our lives and as I have already specified it is ultimately related to the fact that ideas have consequences that permeate into all areas of life, including of course definitions of manhood and womanhood.

The Creation mandate in Genesis 2v15 is a twofold calling to preserve and protect, in short to be 'gatekeepers' of all creation and this applies to all mankind not just the covenant community of Christ. However, have the people of God really understood what it means to carry our glory and honour as men and women in the image of the triune God? We have been bestowed with a glory and an honour and are called to preserve and protect creation then.

Moreover, with the emergence of multiculturalism in a post-colonial world, Roy McCloughry argues that masculinity

*'is not mono-cultural, even within our own
society, since there are several different sub-
cultures even within the world of men'*[28]

Contemporary post-modern culture would argue that masculinity is a social construction and relative. Masculinity is different from maleness which is related to our biology and genetics. I am a male because of my physical anatomy yet this does not make me a man, this does not constitute my masculinity.

This is why it is fundamentally about worldviews and the consequences of ideas about all reality. Masculinity itself is a worldview that has personal, social and theological aspects.

Masculinity is to do with values, beliefs, myths, definitions and expectations of what it means to be a man. Despite there being several different sub-culture's and new western views of masculinity, are there still core underlying beliefs and interpretations of what it means to be a man? Do all men 'feel' in a deep place within their masculine psyche that we are designed to provide, protect and procreate? This is one of the questions that this opens up.

At Mount Sinai when God laid the foundations of a nation and indeed all nations because his Law reflects his holy character and sums up the two greatest commandments to love God with all our heart, soul, mind and strength and to love our neighbour even as we care and have love for ourselves (Matthew 22v37-39). Only by confessing our total helplessness and powerlessness to fulfil the two greatest commandments, and crying out in desperate need for mercy and grace and in repentance for the idols in our hearts that we have used to quench our deep thirst, can we receive and appreciate his grace.

Men have been given this responsibility, to be the foundation of a nation in all areas. The sins of the fathers

[28] Roy McCloughry, *Third Way* Magazine p17-19 October 1992 edition, Vol 15

are about the sins of idolatry as Exodus 20v3-4 specify. In a multicultural, post-colonial, pluralistic society of a whole melting pot of worldviews, I was born, but out of wedlock and had no mother or father as I grew up.

This, along with the lack of true mentors and spiritual fathers in the Church has meant that I have not balanced the four pillars of king, warrior, mentor and friend very well, nor have I lived out of the six aspects that reflect our fundamental purpose, but I 'sense' that these key words encapsulate manhood as God designed it to be, and am trying to be proactive in responding to what I feel called to.

CHAPTER 5

My personal journey of fatherlessness

I was put into a large foster home in the South of England at 8 weeks old with just a foster mother and many children coming and going on a regular basis. My real mother came to England from Trinidad & Tobago, the southern-most Caribbean island. When I was five years old my mother who was something of a stranger to me, took me away from the home and we took a long journey on a boat back to Trinidad.

The first five years of our life lay something of a foundation and we get used to our environment whatever or wherever that may be. I had no foundation, so I had no idea what a man was or how to be a foundation later on in life. This deeply traumatised me and in retrospect it felt like I was effectively kidnapped at such a tender age. I was so distressed, they put me on a plane with a friend of my mother's and I returned to the foster home just six weeks later. It was not until much later that the symptoms of this began to show, namely rootlessness.

Like countless numbers of men, I have never been initiated into manhood and brought into a community of men. Also I have never been mentored, discipled or spiritually fathered in the Church either. These roles then of being a provider, protector and procreator are profoundly alien to me. I have not really even lived much in a masculine world, not an intentional healthy conscious masculine world. There were *no* father figures in my childhood and teenage years. So like many kids who go through the care system, with no boundaries or discipline, I went into rebellion and chaos and began life from age thirteen without a map. I was lost, confused, and insecure.

I had no idea where I was going or what I was doing.

Teenage years.

I started smoking at eleven, and breaking the law from thirteen. I left school with no qualifications at all and I had built up quite a long criminal record by my late teens. Probation served no purpose as I continued to break the law. This was just one of the consequences of having no strong masculine presence in my life, whether that is a real biological father or father figure. There's nothing new under the sun, it's the same today. Why do boys join gangs? They are like surrogate fathers or substitute families.

One of my 'substitute families' was getting into football hooliganism. I followed Chelsea and loved the camaraderie and atmosphere of singing, and the passion I got from cheering on my team. I can see now that the energy of youth was being channelled destructively rather than creatively, but this is what happens with no mentor or guidance. I drank quite heavily and was very angry and confused about who I was or where I really belonged and to who, for I had no foundations at all.

Through the foster home I had social workers up until I was sixteen but never co-operated with them, I just was not interested. I lived literally for the moment. I had a 'long term' girl-friend between fifteen and seventeen years old, which seems a very long time at that age, so I was cut deep when we finished, but I was a mess. I had no prospects without any qualifications and began to do unskilled jobs working in factories and labouring on building sites and I hated every minute of it. In between jobs, I would continue to get in trouble with the police or walk around building sites asking for work or knocking on doors of firms on the local industrial estates.

Adventure

I longed deeply for adventure like most teenagers, so I tried but failed to get into the Merchant Navy but my longing for adventure continued when I hitch hiked around Europe at 19 years old with a friend. We made our way through France and into Germany to live it up at the Munich Beer Festival and then set out to go to Israel to join a kibbutz.

After a very long haul from Munich we arrived in Athens but could not afford the boat fare and so were stranded with about £6 between us. We tried hitching back to Munich during the winter. It was a really gruelling journey as we had to deal with being cold and hungry a lot of the time, so we stole regularly to eat and also tucked into people's left overs. I became a good thief. We were down to our last few pennies. As we arrived at a train station on the way to Zagreb, I stole a wad of cash and we ran down the road singing but were caught immediately and several police beat up on me with truncheons, they broke my hand and it had to heal by itself. We ended up in a communist prison in the old Yugoslavia, in a little town called Sisak near Zagreb, in what is now called Croatia.

My right hand looked so grotesque with the bone sticking out, I was in agony. The hardest thing to deal with apart from the 'food' was that we did not know how long we had to be there. You can learn to adapt but not knowing when it would be over made the day's so unbearably long and torturous. Mercifully I did not get any more beatings in prison.

While I was in prison I prayed for the first time even though I had no intentions on making any decision to give my life to 'God' whoever He was and whatever He was. We were in prison for forty two days and they decided that we had paid for our crime and let us go, it could have been two years.

It does not sound long, but at nineteen in a communist country, it was enough for me thank you very much. This experience in the old Yugoslavia proved to be the catalyst that God used to begin wooing and drawing me to Himself.

The search

After getting back to the UK I met my mother for the first time as an adult, which was a bit surreal initially. It felt like it was too late to salvage a relationship with her, and I am sure it was because we never really bonded or lived together. My heart was shut down toward her even though I was not aware of it. The last time I had seen her was about six years before when I was thirteen and she emigrated to Santa Monica in California with her new husband and their baby, a boy called Mark. She asked me to go with her but I had my own 'life' with my friends and football.

I got turned on to smoking hash when I was in Europe and I was smoking more and more even though I began to search for God. A lifestyle of nomadic rootlessness began to emerge and I simply could not or would not settle in one place. I went from one mundane job to another and from one geographical place to another and this was a pattern that lasted for many years. I had no sense of belonging to anyone, anywhere or anything. This has actually been the case even as a Christian and the healing of the father wound was to be also the healing of not feeling I belong. This is a main characteristic of an 'orphan spirit'.

For about two to three years I searched. I had gone from an angry, confused lost little boy during my teenage years that had joined the tribe of football hooliganism to seeking adventure in Europe, to now writing poetry and walking through the forest which I loved. I began to read a lot as well. I looked into different religions and philosophies. Although I thought I was searching for God, actually it was He who found me, and I came to Christ in 1982.

I had a very real and powerful conversion. I devoured the Bible, was baptised and felt brand new because I was. However, I had no church and subsequently I 'backslid' and got deep into drugs as I integrated into a 'hippie' subculture, which was just another substitute family to me. After five or six years of regular indulgence in the drug scene I repented and God brought me back to himself through a guy I got to know. I went to a local Pentecostal church for a few months but felt so alien and did not like it at all. The people there grew up in the church and they were predominantly white and Middle Class, so there was a definite culture to the church. I was a fish out of water inside the church.

Taste of Missions and 'Family'.

I then joined a missionary organisation called YWAM (Youth With A Mission) and had the best time of my life up to that point. I completed a discipleship training course and became so close with the other Christians on the course. I learnt more of God's Word, and I remember the teaching on the Father Heart of God was particularly meaningful to me, which came as no surprise. I went to South East Asia with a team of seven. We were based mostly in Hong Kong with a Dutch Church planting team, but we started in Manila in the Philippines which I loved more than Hong Kong because they were so warm and friendly.

I experienced poverty like I had never seen before, it was of such stunning intensity that it left us all completely speechless. We tried smuggling bibles into China which I loved planning for because it nourished my longing for adventure, even though two groups of men got caught.. They were fine about it, allowed us one bible and gave us a receipt to pick them up on the way back. The three women on our team got through so we were stuck with three hundred Mandarin bibles and decided to leave them in a hotel in Canton.

I split up from the team and worked on Hong Kong Island with ex-Triad gang members who had been heroin addicts most of their lives, it was hard work but this was like 'home' as well as 'family' and I became really good friends with a couple of American guys while working there. I am still friends with them to this day and even went there to live much later on in my life. I remember standing on Hong Kong Island and saying to God 'I'll go anywhere for you except Horsham' which was my hometown. Guess where I went back to?

Driven into the wilderness

On my return to England, living in my home town and not wanting to be there at all, I attended the local church where I felt so alienated. An emotional pain began to churn within me and it intensified more and more every-day. It became so unbearable; I would break down on the street and wail with blood curdling cries. I was scared because I did not know what was happening to me, and deeply confused because I had just had one of the best years of my life and now I was walking through my own private crisis.

I knew I was born again of the Spirit of God and that I belonged to God, but someone asked me during this time, if anyone had ever prayed about an orphan spirit for me and I said no and thought no more of it. Yet I had no one to pour my heart out to. I was in a desperate state. Emotionally, and psychologically I was edging nearer and nearer to the precipice.

Looking back it reminds me of the famous poem *The Divine Comedy* written by an Italian poet Dante who at thirty five described his travels through Hell, Purgatory and Heaven. I personally do not believe in Purgatory but related deeply to a particular place in the poem. At a deeper level the poem represents allegorically the soul's journey towards God. He gets lost in a Dark Wood assailed by beasts he cannot evade and unable to find the right way. This was me during this time; I was lost in a Dark Wood and felt totally and utterly alone. I was in a howling desolate wasteland and felt like God had left me.

In retrospect, I realise now that the pain of being abruptly cut off again from what felt like a 'family' was just too traumatic and this extreme pain ended with me taking a large overdose as the emotional pain inside was so unbearable. No one knew about it. I had my stomach pumped out, but did not really have anyone to process the intensity of the anguish I was going through, and this was a twofold problem, one because I was totally unaware of the deeper issues of manhood that I had not been initiated and helped with.

This is why I struggled with the church, there was no room or space to be real and there was a subtle pressure to always be 'happy' and 'joyful'. Six months after my overdose, I applied to the missionary organisation again-this time to join a ship that went around the world in a type of mercy ministry, which in retrospect was another attempt to get back to what I saw as my 'family'.

How God 'Initiated' me

While waiting to hear the result of my application, I took a driving job delivering pizzas. Having just passed my driving test, I was looking forward so much to joining the ship, getting back to my friends and for another taste of adventure. On the first day of my driving job, the back tyre blew out. The van was on its side, I could not see my legs, and petrol was leaking everywhere. The first thing I said was 'I guess that's a no then Lord'.

I was not about to go around the world on a missionary ship. Instead of my dream, I was hurled into what felt like a nightmare. Eventually the fire brigade and ambulance arrived and three hours later I emerged out of the wreck not knowing if I would walk again. I was told that I would walk again but would have to live with chronic pain for the rest of my life. The next day they operated and fixed my two broken legs with two long metal rods and lots of screws. I have about twenty seven inches of scars as a result. I was 29 and would never be the same again physically.

Despite a man's past and the failures of his own father to initiate him from boyhood to manhood, God himself can take him on that journey and provide what was missing. So as I look back I know now that God initiated me by driving me into a wilderness which lasted about fifteen to twenty years. The initiation took the form of chronic physical pain that forced me into a deeper more abiding sense of manhood. I learned to 'endure hardship' because God wanted to forge me into a warrior for Him and to cling to Him.

This will sound very strange and even offensive to some Christians depending on their theology, however there is a pattern throughout the Scriptures, when God's Word came to a man, he then began to deal with him and for many years God humbled, refined, matured and built character into the man before His Word was fulfilled. God gave Joseph a dream but he went through many years of being prepared and as Psalm 105v18 says the iron that was around his feet came into his soul.

Abraham waited over twenty years before Isaac was born. Jacob wrestled with the angel after twenty years of God building some character into him before he became 'Israel' a prince with God. After growing up amongst the pleasures of Egypt, Moses was driven into the wilderness to become a humble shepherd but also a mighty prophet. David was anointed as king but was prepared through twenty years of persecution and being hunted down. The Lord himself waited thirty years before his public ministry.

For three months while in hospital I did not even bear weight on my legs. I developed an acute nerve pain in my left foot and for three whole weeks non-stop I screamed out in blood curdling agony. I was drugged up with Pethidine injections and a liquid called Oromorph which was like liquid morphine. I thought I had left drugs behind me but I was going to need strong pain killers for the rest of my life. I left hospital in a wheelchair with two broken legs and two damaged nerves in my left leg.

I had no qualifications at all and I had nowhere really to live, and after an extremely difficult stay at a friend's father's I convalesced at the foster home that I grew up in. I spent a few months there which helped because I was able to relax. I quickly settled into a routine. I slept in the hall with my wheelchair by my side. The ambulance came to collect me at 10am for Physiotherapy and Occupational Therapy which lasted for several months.

The time came for me to get out my wheelchair and try to walk. It was a defining moment and I felt scared. I put my hands onto the parallel bars, pulled myself up and stood. I felt so humbled and somewhat humiliated actually but determined to fight hard. I walked the length of the bars and continued with the help of the physios as I literally poured with sweat. It felt good. I could walk.

It took me 18 months to walk properly without any aids and I was dependent on strong pain killers. Like I said, both nerves in my left leg were damaged and this meant that I would have nerve spasms mostly in my left foot. For about a period of fifteen months I was intensely angry with God and the world in general. As I emerged out of this rage against God, he gently wooed me into his arms through repentance and forgiveness.

I could be grateful though to God for the valley I had gone through, for like Jacob I wrestled with Him through my own dark night of the soul alone (Genesis 32v24-30) Jacob wrestled alone in the dark and actually prevailed in his own strength. Then God struck him on his hip (V25) the strongest part and broke him. It was not until he was broken that he began to cling to God and sought favour from Him 'with tears' (Hosea 12v4) When his strongest part was broken, *then* he was able to 'cling' and it was not until he began to cling that he sought the blessing.

He brings us to our own 'River Jabbok' where it is dark, lonely and feels like we have nothing but God alone, yet there at our own Jabbok God changes our name, meaning our character. Though we may have a spiritual 'limp' and be weakened, it is where our calling as true sons is forged and out of that furnace our calling is crystallised and revealed. Therein was the blessing though, for again like Jacob I began to cling and say 'I will not let You go unless you bless me'.

Getting educated again and God's question

I did not know what I was going to do with my life though. I had no trade, no job, no qualifications, no supportive family; I was pretty much on my own. Just me and God together. After getting out of the wheelchair I spent just over a year on crutches and wore a leg calliper. While I was on crutches I began to look into opportunities to study, so I attended a local College and started to get educated at age thirty. I completed a course in Social Care but I could not get work in this so I went back to College to do another course studying Humanities on what is called an Access to Higher Education course. I loved it and a love for learning began to take root. I stayed with education for quite a long time.

From 1995 God took me in different direction and I became thoroughly immersed in the theology of the 16th century Reformation, so I spent about seven years with the guy who had led me to the Lord, studying and discussing the effects of Reformation theology on culture. This led me to ask a question 'Why did the Church become so peripheral and marginalised to culture'?

I devoured some of Francis Shaeffer's books which helped me to understand the history and roots of the decline in Western culture. I went to Glasgow University to study philosophy, theology and sociology but I quit after the first term and in March 1998 I moved to Albuquerque, New Mexico in the South West of the States to be near to my friends who I had met in Hong Kong.

While I was there my interest in Apologetics (defence of the faith) and Worldviews grew because I felt that I needed to become equipped to engage with contemporary culture. My mind was being deeply enriched, yet this was also the start of my interest in the masculine journey as well, and the stages men go through throughout their life. God spoke to me through Elijah hiding in the cave (1 Kings 19v9,13) and asked me the same question 'What are you doing here Nigel'?

Not what are you doing here physically but what are doing here in this emotional cave. I was becoming grounded doctrinally and intellectually and this has stood me in good stead. However, my heart was still buried and I needed to get it back in order to live from it, not just my head. It was not until a few years later that I began to answer God's question because I spent six years in Higher Education. I began a BA degree in Biblical Studies, had a year in New Mexico and returned to live in England, something I profoundly regretted as I had no one or nothing to come back to.

My mind was becoming sharper but my heart was still un- healed in crucial areas, particularly the orphan heart in me. I had the closest thing to family and love that I had ever experienced when I lived in the States, yet I walked away from it and the emotional anguish I experienced from what felt like the biggest mistake of my life was intense. I tried to get back there three times but it never worked out and each time it failed I was devastated and could not understand why God did not open the way for me. I feared what I longed for and my heart was still so deeply buried.

I finished the BA in Biblical Studies and then spent two years trying to figure out what I wanted to do. I wanted to teach adults but could not get a job teaching theology to adults with a degree from the States; it was not recognised in the UK. I did a second degree in Cultural Studies followed by a teacher training course and became a qualified Fur ther Education teacher of Sociology, six years after I returned from the States.

So there I was a qualified teacher of Sociology after a long and painful journey.Yes I savoured the moment when I qualified especially as I had walked alone through all my fiercest battles and it was hard to not have anyone say to me 'well done, you did good'. I knew that Abba Father had said well done to me though. Not only had the Father said he was proud of me, he spoke to me one day shortly after I qualified and said 'Men carry pictures of their children in their wallets because they delight in them and feel so proud of them, if I had a wallet I would have a picture of you inside it'. This is what I mean by tangible experience of Abba's Love.

The Father's love has meant everything because I could easily have defined and lost myself in being a 'teacher' and hid behind a mask of so called 'professional' status. It had taken over twenty five years to secure an occupation and so it could have so easily become my identity and been the basis of my significance as a man. A lifetime of physical pain and living on the raw edge of my own desperation has kept me grounded to some extent.

Yet the truth is that if life is a raw edge of desperation, you don't live, you survive. Survivors exist, overcomers live. I had been in survival mode my entire life but this is fundamental to abandonment and attachment deficit that goes with an orphan heart. Even though God had said he was proud of me and well done, my heart was still locked into survival thinking which comes from a slave mind-set rather than the freedom of a true son of the Father. There was still much work to be done.

The challenge for me as I believe it is for most men and that is to find our significance, our security, our self-worth that forms our identity from the love and affirmation of the Father before we *do* anything. Just as Jesus was affirmed as the Beloved Son at his baptism before he said or did anything, so we too (men and women) can find our significance, security and self-worth from a place of rest in the Father's love and affirmation as we nestle in his bosom rather than wrestle with him by perceiving His heart through the cracked mirror of our brokenness. Like the blind man who Jesus led by the hand out of the village and saw 'men like trees walking' so I was progressively seeing.

In the five years of being a Further Education teacher, I have only experienced one full year of actual teaching though. I have been unemployed for four years and this has been really tough to say the least, but I have had the opportunity to ask Jesus to come and rescue my heart, awaken it, heal it and set it free. It has given me the chance and the time to explore and let God bring to the surface the particular pieces of my buried heart with all of its broken dreams and pain, rather than avoid it, by staying in survival mode. It was God saying to me 'it's time to come out of the cave' and live. The longing for a cause to live for, to experience a deep sense of calling began to be insatiable and still is.

Season of healing and the Father's Embrace

I went to India to explore an opportunity to teach at a School of Humanities with the same missionary organisation I was with over twenty years ago in Hong Kong. This School was based on apologetics and worldviews and it seemed to be a niche. However, the place was way too secluded and monastic for me and I knew with conviction that this was not right, but I met a guy called Brian there who had started a mission ten years ago with his wife in Kathmandu in Nepal and we really gelled.

Three years later (in between a heart attack in July 2008) I spent a month with their team and this was to be significantly related to what I believed to be a calling. I was only at this mission base in India for three weeks, but while I was there I also met some people who were from a ministry called The Fathers Love based in Malaysia and my time spent with them was crucial because Abba Father was wooing me into his arms to experience his embrace. I remember a book entitled *'Experiencing the Father's Embrace'* and this was to be core to the healing of my heart and of my manhood.

When I returned it was if I went into the very depths of my own cave emotionally and spiritually. I sank to one of the lowest points in my life. Like a master surgeon though God exposed some of the deepest wounds, and this culminated in an actual heart attack, which was genetic. If the physical is a reflection on the spiritual then my heart was feeling rather fragmented, but Aslan (Jesus) was on the move. I had begun a season of healing before I went to India, and this was another reason it was not right for me to work there with the mission.

This season continued on my return but God took me into the deepest core of unresolved trauma, right back to the moment of conception, through my birth, the first five years especially and I invited Him to walk with me through the different stages of my life. It was a process of Him exposing and surfacing the buried toxic pain that I had hid behind through inner vows and my own unique fig leaves to hide exposure of my 'naked' pain, shame, guilt, fears and blame.

Whether we are 'In Adam' or 'In Christ' we can still be stuck in an 'Adam and Eve' complex of hiding from our own 'nakedness' through fear, shame and blame. Jesus said the world would respond in a particular way because they observed something about his followers, which was his love. So the way that his people loved each other, the world would know that they belong to Jesus (John 13v35). Now why does the world tend to not respond in this way? Why do people not ask followers of Jesus a reason for the hope that is in them? (1 Peter 3v15).

Love and Hope should so characterise us in such a way that it causes a reaction from those who don't know Him. If we don't love each other in this way it is probably because too many people are bound up by fear, because God's perfect love drives out fear (1 John 4v18). Do you know anyone who is characterised by such a radical love and such a contagious hope that people automatically know they are disciples of Jesus? Are we ourselves such a person?

Anyway as I let go of the buried toxic pain from my childhood and what I did'nt get from parents, my spirit became lighter and I did not need to take 'the meds' anymore, meaning if we are being healed then we won't need to indulge in whatever numbs the pain, which will be our own addiction. It is about being intentional but we are all at a different place in our lives according to our unique personality, temperament and past. I had shifted my allegiance and chosen life instead of death.

As Gordon Dalbey who pioneered the Christian men's movement in the 1980s with his book *Healing the Masculine Soul* says *'Humble before God, Fierce toward the enemy, and real before men'.* I just did not want to go through life merely surviving any longer. It was about doing the work that I needed to do in order to live in the reality of my spiritual inheritance, anointing, authority, calling and destiny. These are some of the key themes of what I was in pursuit of, the key words that capture my deepest longing and still do.

On the first page of my journal at the time I had written a quote from Gordon Dalbey *'The flak is thickest when you're over the target. The intensity of the resistance that is, often measures the significance of God's call'.* This came from a men's conference I had attended shortly after I had re-located to pursue this season of healing. It was going to be a fight to get my true masculine heart back, there is an enemy who lies to us and steals our true identity, kills our heart and destroys our future, but I was up for it, life is too short to merely cope.

At the men's conference a hundred men stood in a circle with their arms around each other's shoulders singing 'lean on me when you're not strong, and I'll be your friend, I'll help you carry on, just lean on me brother when you need a hand, we all need somebody to lean on'. It was truly inspiring and speaks into my deepest dreams. I remember standing at a well-known local nature spot, and looking out at a breathtakingly beautiful scene overlooking the Sussex Downs near to where I was living at the time, just before I re-located, and declared to God 'I dare to dream God, I dare to still dream'. I had to go after it though.

The Father's Embrace was essential to my healing.

I began to hear God's voice more as I became real with how I *really* felt about my life. The releasing of the toxic pain, and the dismantling of the walls of self-protection and deep denial in my heart created more space to hear his whisper. I sensed that the Father wanted to embrace me, but as I stepped into the Fathers welcome and Embrace, How did I imagine it? A celebration? A garden full of his presence? A mansion with my name on it? A rebuke for all my failures? How do we imagine that tailor made welcome just for us?

How does the Father deal with our stench from our own pig pen? He does not turn us away. I had to imagine that my true self breathing and growing more deeply in the Father's Embrace, in the acknowledgment of who he created me to be. The current areas of unresolved brokenness and sin make up our pig pen but the audacity of our false self begins to wither away in the Father's Embrace and presence. Some of the darkness lifts because our true self grows.

So I imagined my true self flourishing in the Father's Welcome. I asked the Father a question one day. I wrote in journal (quote) 'What does your tailor made Embrace look like for me Father'? Immediately the image of Dorothy in

The Wizard of Oz holding her dog and clicking her heels saying 'There's no place like home, there's no place like home' (unquote) The Father was saying to me effectively 'My Embrace is your true home, I am your true home'. Also the Father reminded me that in this film The Tin Man was looking for his heart. I was so longing to have my true masculine heart back so that I could love the Father but also pursue and love the right woman.

Henri Nouwen said 'Trust is that deep inner conviction that the Father wants me home'. The epidemic of Father absence creates a deep inability to trust God I believe, and we then project onto him and others, our own pain. It's a combination of emotional wounds and the lies of the enemy. Ultimately the reason people don't seem to ask Christians about the Hope that is in them is because this root issue of Father absence is a spiritual issue. There has been such a focused demonic assault on the family through generational fatherlessness that men have been taken out in an incomprehensible way, as well as women. It's as if men are walking around under some kind of spell and it is a monstrous enchantment because it means we don't know who we really are.

Then he spoke to me through a moment in the Lion, the Witch and the Wardrobe when Aslan commissioned Peter and I believe this relates to the call he has on my life. Moreover there came another moment when they realised that 'Aslan was on the move'. Jesus was on the move coming for my heart. In fact during this season of healing and restoration, God began to speak to me much more through specific scenes in films and this penetrated into my spirit as He was wooing and dismantling the walls of self-protection through his tenderness.

This way of getting through to me was also symbolic and visual and these scenes are embedded in my heart. The tenderness of Almighty God slays me and wrecks me, and I am so grateful to Him for his tenderness. God can speak through anything or anyone, needless to say though, the Word and the Spirit work together.

The Father's Embrace then as in the story of the Prodigal was to be absolutely crucial to the rescue, the redemption, restoration, healing and freedom of my true heart and it will remain to be crucial for the rest of my journey, simply because I was created by Love for Love. Tangible experience of Abba Fathers Embrace and love through His Word and Spirit, his people, in whatever ways he chooses to tell me that I am his Beloved, has been a necessary on-going reality.

1 John 4v18-19 implies that we cannot cast out our fears but we have to *displace* them by introducing the orphan heart to Love that is perfect, but we must then make a choice to either risk opening up our heart and submitting to perfect Love or continue to put up walls of self-protection. In short, we either build a bridge or a wall.

The deep restoration and rescue of my buried heart could not occur in isolation, for true healing only happens in the context of safe, healthy and authentic relationships that are intentional, and yet this is what I been searching for and unless we are intentional about it, we simply go through the motions of Church life. Men need this naked transparency with each other and with God in order to come out of our various caves.

Healing, Discipleship, Counselling and Warfare have all been a part of my journey but in a spasmodic and infrequent manner and in different locations. This is not ideal and although from the orphan heart in me I constantly moved from place to place in search of these four aspects. Healing and freedom has to happen in authentic relationships, even though the Father's Embrace for me has occurred in times of my greatest anguish and heart wrenching excruciating agony.

The process of displacing orphan thinking in me gave birth to a hope I had not experienced before, I began to dream again and believe, so I have been on a journey to pursue His calling on my life, and this is what has emerged out of an intentional season of healing to cut the roots of the toxic pain within that kept me in my own cave. 'What are you doing here Elijah' God asked. His question became powerfully relevant, but even more the two reasons that God gave Elijah to come out of his cave. 'Go back to the calling I gave you and be a mentor to a younger man'. (1 Kings 19v 15-16)

We are called to advance a magnificent Kingdom, to be kings, priests, warriors, prophets, mentors and spiritual fathers, to live in an Epic Story and not go missing in action in isolated cocoons of self-comfort. First though, we need an encounter with who the Father really is. So we can get to a place of rest in the Father's love and thus live from deep approval and affirmation as true sons not as slaves of religion or institutional Church-ianity that tames the wildness, fierceness and tenderness that reflects a biblical balance of both Lamb and Lion.

We need to experientially become the Beloved sons of the Father because fear and uncertainty about who we really are in Christ has also kept us in our caves as well as the generational father wound that stems from father absence. God took me on a journey to heal me of the effects of a father wound in particular; it has been and still is through the Father's Embrace and becoming a beloved son of Abba.

CHAPTER 6

Becoming the Beloved of God

Through The Fathers Embrace

It is important to emphasise here, that although becoming the Beloved of God in this chapter will appear of an overly subjective nature and although a personal encounter with Jesus is necessary, but we do not believe simply because he lives in our hearts (John 14v23; 1 Corinthians 3v16). This could be interpreted as a kind of Neo-Gnosticism or mysticism which neglects God's objective, historic revelation in Creation, Scripture and Christ. If we begin with experience at the expense of God's revelation – we will be on a foundation of sand for this historically has led to error. It is the same today; there is nothing new under the sun. I am most definitely *not* presenting any form of inner subjective revelation at the expense of the Scriptures here.

We believe because Christ truly came, truly suffered, truly died, and truly rose again for our Justification (1 Corinthians 15v3-8). The other side of the coin of Justification which is Adoption has been seriously neglected though. For this is where the Judge steps down out of his courtly robes, picks us up, takes us home and becomes our Abba, Father. We have to get out of the 'court room' and into the warmth of the 'living room' where we can sit in front of a roaring log fire so to speak and be totally free to be our true selves before our Abba.

The Ultimate Orphan Maker – the enemy of God.

The historical Father Absence that can be traced as far back to before the Industrial Revolution in the modern era is not a cultural phenomenon. In tracing the true roots of the orphan condition of human beings, from a biblical perspective, the orphan condition has its origins before time began. As the saying goes 'a text without a con-text is a con'. The following term used by the Lord Jesus to his disciples 'I will not leave you as orphans' (John 14v18) as he prepared himself for His sufferings will help if it is viewed in the wider context of the whole counsel of God. The Lord could have used any number of words yet he used the word 'orphans'. Why?

There was war in heaven before the creation of the world (Revelation 12v7-13), the biblical worldview therefore is a warfare worldview. The archangel Lucifer instead of living and serving in heaven before the throne of the Father, rebelled against the Father and was cast out of heaven to the earth. He became the arch enemy of God and the first thing he did was to seek vengeance and retaliate against God by destroying what God had made, a creature made in the likeness and image of God himself.

The love and unity within the Trinity was meant to be shared by us (John 17v25-26) We are made in the very image and likeness of God (Genesis 1v26-28; Psalm 8v5) so we are 'crowned with glory and honour', and the enemy hates the glory of God that is hidden in our hearts because we have what he wanted. The glory is in our hearts for Christ is in us 'the hope of glory' and it is God 'who has shone in our hearts to give the light of the knowledge of the glory of God in the face of Jesus Christ' (Colossians 1v27b; 2 Corinthians 4v6). It is so crucial to know who we really are as beloved sons of the Father crowned with glory.

However, Lucifer who became Satan meaning 'adversary' chose of his own free will to become the Ultimate

Orphan and thus the ultimate orphan maker. The enemy seeks to destroy nations, and nations are made up of families of men, women and children. He has specifically stolen and sought to destroy our true identity, as *image bearers* in creation and as *beloved sons* in our redemption.

Through his lies and deception in particular, even as born again believers, it seems we have been vague about our true identity. The enemy knows who we really are, God knows who we really are, even Creation itself knows who we really are for it 'eagerly waits for the revealing of the sons of God' (Romans 8v19) Do we know who we really are as both image bearers and beloved sons of the Father or have we allowed the enemy to commit 'identity theft' on us?

Man's dignity and nobility in Creation.

In the first six days of creation God forms then fills the physical universe and so he provides for what is to come. It is as if Genesis 1v26 is the culmination of all that has gone before as God announces his plan ahead of time when the members of the Trinity consult with each other 'Let Us make man in Our image, according to our likeness'. He creates the first human couple to have dominion over the earth and to govern it in his name. Clearly, humans are not the supreme rulers of creation or totally autonomous in their freedom to do whatever they wish. Our dominion is a delegated authority and so we are called to be representatives or ambassadors of the Supreme Ruler of Creation, God.

Genesis 1v26-27 conveys the reason for being for humans, male and female (God said to 'them') and the fundamental aspect of human identity, the image of God. When God created us in his own image and likeness he 'saw everything that he had made, and indeed it was very good' (Genesis 1v31), and despite the messages of our wounds or the dark voices, no one can ever change the immense value and dignity of who we really are. Genesis chapter one comes before chapter three.

As Nancy Pearcey says 'In Genesis, God gives what we might call the first job description':

> *'Be fruitful and multiply and fill the earth and subdue it'. The first phrase 'be fr uitful and multiply', means to develop the social world: build families, churches, schools, cities, governments, laws. The second phrase 'subdue the earth' means to harness the natural world: plant crops, build bridges, design computers, and compose music. This passage is sometimes called the Cultural Mandate because it tells us our original purpose was to create cultures, build civilisations; nothing less...the way we serve a Creator God is by being creative with the talents and gifts He has given us'* [29]

So we have been made a 'little lower than God and crowned with glory and honour, and have been given dominion over all the works of God's hands, with all things under our feet' and so were designed to be co-workers and stewards of creation. The image of God means that we are like him as relational, social, communal, volitional, moral, spiritual, emotional, reasoning and creative beings. The word glory means 'weight' or substance and this also refers not only to our origins generally, but also relates to our own individual uniqueness and what we feel stirred and called to pursue in relation to our giftedness in the sphere of influence God has equipped us for.

So Adam and Eve had to establish an environment in which they could grow and increase in number. Work then

---

[29] Nancy Pearcey, *Total Truth, liberating Christianity from its cultural captivity* (Crossway Books, 2005) p.47

comes *before* the Fall and therefore *before* sin and death enter the world and they hide from their Maker. This implies that work is not a part of the curse; it is what God designed us for because we were made to bear fruit. Modern life however has become so dominated by the demands of work that it seriously damages the image of God in us; this is because we are fundamentally relational and communal beings just like God himself within the Godhead.

Too much work has the potential to destroy relationships and even family and community and this relates also to the characteristics of a Babylonian pagan culture, for amongst all of the things that are traded in Babylon are the *'bodies and souls of men'* (Revelation 18v13). This speaks of just how brutal and comprehensive the effects of an unfettered free market without regulation has been on families, communities and nations, not to mention the ecological, ethical and economical rupture that this rampant individual greed of the wealthiest has created in modern life.

Mike Breen states that

> *'This is not what God had in mind when he made us to be fruitful. God designed us to be productive. But we misunderstand what that means. We build our identities around our activities. We have become human 'doings' rather human 'beings' especially in Western culture. We've got the whole thing backward. A biblical framework for a rhythm of life allows us to be fruitful in balance with being at rest. We need to be secure in who we are, based on what Christ did for us on the cross and the very great promises we have that we are loved and accepted by God. We must put the brakes on living a driven lifestyle'* [30]

---

[30] Mike Breen and Walt Kallestad, *A Passionate Life* (Cook Communications Ministries) p.62-3

Being productive is basic to bearing the image of God but not at the expense of damaging our bodies, souls and relationships with both God and others. He goes on to point out that the commandment to keep the Sabbath is right up there with 'Don't kill, don't steal, and don't commit adultery'. In other words he says that being a workaholic is, to God, just as bad as being a murderer or adultery. That sounds rather a strong thing to say, but *rest* is key to loving God and loving our neighbour as ourselves. This means that as human beings we must start from a place of rest to fulfil our calling to be fruitful. Resting in God, abiding in his presence-is the only way we can be successful in what he has called us to do.

Having been formed and created in the image of God himself with everything that entails which reveals our innate dignity and nobility in creation, but in redemption our dignity and nobility is even greater, for we are the very beloved of God. Moreover, in redemption the cost was the sacrifice of God's Son. This means that having a deep, experiential and intuitive understanding of our true son-ship determines whether we come into our true calling, purpose and destiny. We tend to automatically link the topic of 'Calling' with God's will. Being in the centre of His will can then become obsessive and so we fear missing his will and that we have disobeyed him.

Fear of missing God's will can stem from a distorted image of God as the demanding, punishing Father, and so in our fearful, childish and wounded hearts we wrongly conclude that the hardships of our life must be God's punishment for somehow having disobeyed him. The Word of God is clear that this fear is rooted in a sense of not being loved.

As John declares 'There is no fear in love, but perfect love casts out fear, because fear involves torment. But he who fears has not been made perfect in love' (1 John 4v18). When we know in our heart of hearts that we are profoundly, intensely, unconditionally loved by the Father, we are free to fail, free to make mistakes, free to live the adventure that he wants for us. As Augustine said 'Love God, and do what you will'. The legalistic mind-set will automatically object to this, simply because legalism is about fear and bondage.

The love and unity within the Trinity was meant to be shared by us (John 17v25-26) Being beloved sons of the Father is what God himself has accomplished through the life, death, burial, resurrection, ascension, glorification and intercession of the Lord Jesus Christ. We are 'In Christ' and Christ is in the bosom of the Father (John 1v18) so we are also 'in the bosom of the Father'.

Being beloved sons of the Father comes *before* we can be spiritual father.

In this book I have mentioned the need for mentors and spiritual fathers. However, no one can be a father who has not first been a son. No one can be a mother who has not first been a daughter. Obviously Son-ship begins in the natural but many have been deeply wounded by their fathers in a variety of different ways, and unless we have walked through the heart wrenching process of deep heartfelt forgiveness toward our mother's and father's if that is what we need to do, then we are not ready to be a spiritual father because we will still have unresolved emotional baggage that we need to let go of.

Jack Frost in his book on *Spiritual Slavery to Spiritual Son- ship* gives an example from a man called Jack Winter who many considered to be a spiritual father to them. Frost quotes him

> *'I do not want to be anyone's father. I want to focus my life upon what Jesus focused his life upon; Jesus focused His life upon being a son. Until I am more secure in being a son, I think I would just like to focus my life there.*

He went on to say 'When you focus your life on being a leader, it becomes very easy to become controlling and authoritarian. That is a characteristic of an orphan heart. Then you produce children after your kind. Instead, why don't we all start focusing on being a son or daughter who seeks to do only what the Father does, and lives to serve, honour, and bless others? When you do this, people around you will start living and acting like sons and daughters too'. [31]

This means that it is necessary to focus on being sons and daughters of Abba Father which is a heart attitude of submission and recognises its need to be interdependent rather than independent. It means our hearts need to be rooted and grounded in the bosom of the Father, so that we are living and functioning from a place of rest in Abba Father's love. This has to come first before we do or say anything. It also comes before we discover our calling.

At his baptism the Lord Jesus heard the voice of the Father saying 'You are My Beloved Son, in You I am well pleased' (Luke 3v22) The Father spoke from his own Word (Ps 2v7) and the Holy Spirit also descended in tangible form like a dove. So we need both Word and Spirit in a tangible experience of Abba Fathers outrageous, ferocious love. Jesus' heart Brennan Manning said was 'seized with the power of a great affection'. We also need this experience with Abba. Being the Beloved of the Father was what enabled him to face the devil in the wilderness shortly after, because his identity as the Son was tested, his mission and calling was tested but he was able to resist (Luke 4v13), stand firm and return in the power of the Spirit.

---

[31] Jack Frost, *Slavery to Son-ship, your destiny awaits you* (Destiny Image Publishers, 2006) p.157

Communion, community, and ministry are intrinsic for us to become the Beloved because they speak about Jesus.

Shortly after he began his ministry, Jesus went up a mountain to pray all night to the Father and this speaks of his *communion* with the Father (Luke 6v12) He then began to form *community* by choosing twelve disciples who he also named (Luke 6v13) Finally, they began to *minister* to the crowds (Luke 6v17-19). Intimate communion with Abba in a tangible experience that heals and liberates us to rest secure in his bosom must come first.

Christ is in the bosom of the Father (John 1v18), we are in Christ, so where are we? In the bosom of the Father, but we need to emotionally connect with this truth. Christ is the way to the Father, He is the Truth that sets us free from our own striving and subtle forms of legalism and reveals the Father and He is the Life which means that he wants us to know intimately the same love and relationship that is shared between the Father and the Son (John 15v9) which the Holy Spirit will minister to us (Romans 8v15-16). Without relationship there is no life but we need to tangibly experience the same love the Father has for the Son (John 15v9; 1 John 4v16).

Communion with the Father therefore is the basis for true authentic *community* which means common-unity. When we know by first-hand transformative experience that we are the Beloved sons and daughters of God because we have experienced his love and rely on it (1 John 4v16) this affects our relationships with each other. For we will want others to become the Beloved of Abba Father, so others will see that the love we have for each other is based on being the Beloved of God.

Then we can minister to others in a way that does not strive because we are resting in the bosom of the Father so that we work and minister *from* deep approval not *for* approval and this makes all the difference. Jesus focused his life on being a Son, which enabled him to form authentic community and in turn enabled and empowered his community to minister out of this bedrock foundation.

The Father ministered his father heart to me once when he spoke through a scene in the film *Braveheart*. There were four men feeling totally exhausted after a fierce battle but the oldest one was laying on the ground being held and comforted by his son, a fierce warrior. He said 'Son I am dying, and I have lived to become proud of the man you have become'. I can die a happy man'. The son wept, the other two were moved deeply.

This was a father's affirmation to his son at such a crucial moment, a defining moment or a tipping point as it is called. I was undone, and this caused me to weep from the depths of my being because I knew that Abba Father was speaking to me saying 'I am proud of the man you have become' and that has absorbed into my spirit, it is anchored in my heart and nothing and no one can shake that.

Hearing his whisper shifted and realigned my heart to his love in a way I had not known before, all the academic theology I had learnt before this could not be compared with experiencing that crucial shift within through a deep knowing that I am loved no matter what. Have we become so familiar with certain words and truths that they fail to impact and transform us in the way they were meant to? The importance of this emotional connection with the Father's love cannot be emphasised enough because knowing the right doctrine intellectually simply does not heal the heart. Going to church, believing the right things, or going to lots of meetings does not heal your heart. However crucial doctrine is, God is not a doctrine like a cold mathematical equation.

No one had ever told me that they were proud of me before in my entire life, but the King of the Universe spoke it right into my heart. Nothing can take this away from me and nothing whatsoever can compare with it. It was between me and my Abba Father, my strong big Daddy. The Father is waiting to run to us. The indescribable intensity of the love of God for us comes in its most powerful form visibly and audibly in Jesus Christ of Nazareth.

In Ephesians 3v16-19 the Apostle Paul prays for all believers when he asks that the Father would grant us to be strengthened with might by His Spirit in our inner man, that Christ may dwell (make his home) in our hearts through faith, and that you being rooted and grounded in love, may be able to comprehend with all the saints the width, and length, and depth and height, to know the love of Christ what passes knowledge, that you may be filled with all the fullness of God'.

Jesus taught us to pray 'Our Father'. In that culture at that time, it was a radical and revolutionary thing to say. The Greeks were known for standing around and intellectualising about reality and everything. 'God' to the Greeks was a detached impersonal, abstract idea like the 'Uncaused cause, or the immovable mover' as Aristotle referred to God. The Hebrew prophets of the Old Testament spoke of God in warmer terms but only Jesus referred to God in the same way that a little baby speaks to his 'da da' daddy.

To those who interpret everything through cold logic and reason, this would sound rather sentimental probably, but the point is unless we humble ourselves and become like a little child we cannot even see the kingdom of heaven (Matthew 18v3-4). Because Jesus taught us to pray to God as 'Abba' which means 'daddy, papa' it means that He is totally unique and so is our relationship with the King of the Universe.

Brennan Manning asks

'Is your own personal prayer life characterised by the simplicity, childlike candour, boundless trust, and easy familiarity of a little one

crawling up in Daddy's lap? An assured
knowing that the daddy does'nt care if the
child falls asleep, starts playing with toys, or
even starts chatting with little friends, because
the daddy knows the child has essentially
chosen to be with him for that moment? Is
that the spirit of your interior life'? [32]

Of course there are times when the message from the Arrows of the wounds we have taken in our life will speak much louder and feel so much more real than God's love. Another time as I mentioned above, I asked the Father 'What does your tailor made Embrace look like for me personally right now'? Immediately the scene in the film *Wizard of Oz* where Dorothy is clicking her heels holding her little dog and saying 'There's no place like home, there's no place like home'.

The Father was saying to me, I am your home. Orphans don't feel that they belong anywhere or to anyone but I knew from that moment that my whole being belonged to Him, that the Fathers Embrace was my true and real home. A real Home is a place of welcoming love, non-judgmental acceptance, where you can be totally yourself and nourished in every way. This is what the Father's love is, our true home.

We all need a homecoming to Abba Father's Embrace. Jesus showed us in the most famous Parable how God longs to relate to us, by running to us because of his intense compassion, throwing himself on us and kissing us, but much more than this, he has a robe, a ring and shoes for our feet. What do these mean? Mark Stibbe in I Am Your Father says about the ring 'It signified the son's position.

It told everyone about his identity and his authority. Stibbe points out

---

[32] Brennan Manning, *The Furious Longing of God* (David C Cook, 2009) p.44

'To anyone who saw this ring, it said, 'This boy is the father's son' and 'This boy has the authority and the right to make decisions and to give orders around his father's estate'. The father's act of returning the ring is just as special as the giving of the robe. If the robe said 'You're forgiven, the ring say's 'You're family'. As if to emphasise his son's freedom, the father gives his boy a new pair of shoes. The father sends a very clear signal through the gift of these shoes. His boy wanted to embrace the life of a slave or a servant, but the father wants him to embrace the life of a son, of a free man'. The robe say's 'You're forgiven'. The ring say's 'You're family'. The shoes say 'You're free'. [33]

The Prodigal son, the younger one who was a slave to sin, knew he needed to come home, but it was the remembered and valued son-ship that finally persuaded him to turn back to the Father, so even in the pigsty of his failure, sin and brokenness, he knew he was a son (Luke 15v17-18) So it was the loss of everything that brought him to the bottom line of his true identity. It seems that the Prodigal had to lose everything to come into touch with the very ground of his being so to speak, and it was the realisation of his son-ship that became the basis of his choice to live instead of die.

Once he had come in touch with the truth of his son-ship, he could once again hear the voice calling him the Beloved and *feel* the touch of Blessing. Are we driven by our love hungry hearts to seek ways of gaining a sense of self-worth? We have been created by Love, for Love, so if we are not perfected in Abba Father's love, we will try to fill the inevitable and restless vacuum. As Augustine said *'You*

---

[33] Mark Stibbe, *I Am Your Father* (Monarch Books, 2010) p.234-5

have made us for yourself and our hearts our restless until they find their rest in you'.

No human being, no intimate human relationship, no friendship, no community can ever ultimately satisfy the deep needs of our wayward hearts. Because of the deep orphan condition of the human heart as a result of the Fall of man, we are constantly tempted to wallow in our own lostness and lose touch with not only our original glory in Creation as image bearers and thus our God-given humanity but also our basic blessedness as adopted and beloved sons of the Father.

Although the younger son on his return home to the Father prepared a speech which opens up questions of how genuine his repentance really was. He was prepared to be a 'hired servant' because he believed that he was no longer worthy to be called a son (Luke 15v19). Actually all of us can relate to this if we are ruthlessly honest with ourselves and with God. On the way home to the Father then, we can also subconsciously accept the status of a 'hired servant' so at least we can 'survive'. This is rooted in a false belief and distortion of the Father's heart, namely that we can still live as though the Father to whom we are returning demands an explanation. So still clinging to our own sense of worthlessness because of our past sin, wounds or failure, we accept a place that is far below that of a true son. Heart belief in total absolute forgiveness does not come easy does it? It is because basically we are still not able to believe that grace is always greater than our failures.

The distance then between turning around in our own pigsty of sin, failure, brokenness, respectable religiosity of the elder brother, or the façade of Churchianity, and arriving at home to welcome the Father's Embrace involves the journey of being able to humble ourselves as a little boy or little girl to a Big Daddy. Becoming a child to claim our full dignity as sons, is like living and experiencing the joys of a second childhood seen in the Beatitudes.

The words that Jesus spoke at the Lord's Supper relate to our becoming the Beloved. Jesus **Took, Blessed, Broke** *and* **Gave** Becoming the Beloved of God is our top priority for both those outside the Church and those inside because there are many spiritual orphans as well as physical. Of course there are political and social strategies for dealing with the epidemic of fatherlessness but people including many Christians need a revelation of the Father's love for them, they need to feel Abba Father's Embrace and affirmation.

The root issues are spiritual, and God's people are equipped to deal with it at a spiritual level. It will take warfare, healing, counselling, true discipleship, spiritual fathering and mentoring, but God so loved the world that he gave his only begotten Son, therefore he longs to embrace us and to Father us where we have not been fathered. Communion with God as Abba Father will take a season of commitment to letting God love us. The four aspects of eating the bread and wine relate to becoming the Beloved sons and daughters of Abba Father.

We are *Taken* or Chosen by God and when we our spirits connect with our chosen-ness a place in our hearts opens up and a capacity to be able to rest in the Father's love takes root. He chose us in Christ before he created the universe (Ephesians 1v4) The Father has *blessed* us with every spiritual blessing in the heavenly places in Christ, we are chosen in Christ before the creation of the world, adopted from eternity, and accepted in the Beloved, so we are also his Beloved. It actually gave the Father intense pleasure to adopt us as his sons. We are to claim our blessing and then give the blessing to others by saying and ministering to them that they are the Beloved of God.

Our *brokenness* is to do with our relationships, so we have all been broken to a lesser or greater degree in our human relationships. We come face to face with our own brokenness in our time in the desert. It is what we do with our brokenness that determines whether or not we become the Beloved or not. Firstly, we will need courage to embrace our brokenness, and not deny it or hide from it, we need to befriend it and have kindness and compassion on ourselves.

Secondly, dare to put your brokenness under the Blessing that says 'You are My Beloved son/daughter. As we choose to humble ourselves like a child and effectively become as a little boy or girl before a Big Daddy, and be very real with how we really feel and to have the courage to ask 'Father bring my broken areas to the surface' and a bigger space opens up in our hearts to receive the love of the Father.

When we can do this, when we can see with the eyes of our heart that the Father chose us in Christ before time began, and that we are Blessed of the Father as we tangibly experience the Father's love through his Word and Spirit, our hearts open up and we are enabled by his grace to submit our brokenness and let go of it as it becomes absorbed into our Belovedness and a much larger Story than we have previously been living in.

Then we can *Give* and become food and drink for others and we will then be fruitful and will be able to trust the Father, that the deep heart change within us that is able to produce the kind of fruit that will last, the fruit of the Father's love. When we get to the place where we can be fruitful out of our Belovedness we can gain more clarity about our calling.

Resting in the Father's bosom we live *from* approval and affirmation not *for* approval or acceptance, so we will not have to strive and live like the Prodigal's elder brother who was more concerned with being right than having a relationship with the Father. Intimacy and fruitfulness are like two sides of the same coin, however intimacy with Abba Father comes first, and then the natural organic overflow that comes out of this.

CHAPTER 7

Finding and Living out our Calling

A walk with a brother in Kathmandu

We had just come out of a prayer meeting in Kathmandu, in Nepal, and my friend Brian and I were just walking along talking. Brian and his wife Ruth founded The Agape Mission International. The three areas they work in are women at risk, children at risk and leadership development. However, this walk turned out to be one of the defining moments in life that you look back on as crucial to what follows.

It was a time of deep fellowship where we shared our hearts and our desires. Then Brian suddenly said 'Its like an Emmaus Road walk' mainly for the reason that our hearts burned within us as we talked about what we felt God had called us to. Brian then asked me if I would like to write up a curriculum or a course on masculinity but related to our calling. I wrote up a six week course and now this book is also a result of that 'Emmaus Road' walk in Kathmandu.

I told him that I felt called to speak and minister to the hearts of men, mostly broken men, fatherhood and the effects of fatherlessness and how this prevents men from living out what God calls us to. In many ways I in no way feel qualified for this, but it has been said that God does not call the qualified, rather he qualifies the call. What we sense and feel called to is often organic to our life's journey, and one of the great truths that comes out of this organic nature to our calling, is that the greatest area of our brokenness, is often the greatest area of our gifting and anointing, and therefore the greatest of what we have to offer others.

John Eldredge points this out in *Wild at Heart*

> *'Until we are broken, our life will be self-centred, self- reliant; our strength will be our own. So long as you think you are really something in and of yourself, what will you need God for? Only when we enter our wound will we discover our tr ue glor y. As Bly say's 'Where a man's wound is, that is where his genius will be'. There are two reasons for this. First, because the wound was given in the place of your true strength, as an effor t to take you out. Until you go there you are still posing, offering something more shallow and insubstantial. And therefore, second, it is out of your brokenness that you discover what you have to offer the community'. When we begin to offer not merely our gifts but our tr ue selves, that is when we become powerful. That is when we are ready for battle'.* [34]

My area happened to be an orphan spirit and so I feel called to work for the cause of fatherlessness, to somehow leave my mark on the world, and ultimately by God's grace, to leave a legacy. So I did a two day teaching stint to the leadership team on the subject of calling, which also included how the wounds of our past can keep us stuck in different kinds of caves.

So this book came out of a season of healing, out of which I felt compelled to pursue what I felt stirred to do, which entailed a month trip to work with The Agape Mission

---

[34] John Eldredge, *Wild at Heart* (Thomas Nelson, 2001) p.137-8

International in Kathmandu, which I am also a part of, but based in the UK. The deep longing that was birthed in my heart as Jesus began to set the captive free, is still with me and it is this *longing* that has been formed out of this season of healing I was on, as I spent time in the 'belly of the whale' and journeyed into the brokenness that I have talked about.

Psalm 84v2 says 'My soul longs, yes even faints for the courts of the LORD; My heart and my flesh cry out for the living God'.

Mike Bickle says that

> *'A longing is an ache of the heart. It is a cavity of the spirit crying to be filled. In its deepest sense it is neither a tr ue verb nor a tr ue noun, but combines the two, spanning the gap between emotion and genuine need. It is an intangible feeling that ebbs and flows, yet it is a concrete reality. It cannot be reasoned with, negated or dismissed. If not attended to, it will overtake us. One way or another, whether legitimately or illegitimately, a human longing will be filled. It must be'* [35]

God intentionally planted desires deep in our hearts that only he can fulfil, so he designed our hearts to find our deepest satisfaction in him alone and this design in our beings is evident that he is a jealous God who does not want us to be given over to any lesser pleasure than what we were actually made for. We were made for *God*.

Because of the deep intense longings in our hearts, longings to be enjoyed by God, for beauty, for greatness, fascination, intimacy without shame, to be wholehearted, to make an impact and much more. How deep is the longing in the human heart? We have longings, desires, however,

---

[35] Mike Bickle and Deborah Hiebert *The Seven Longings of the Human Heart* (Forerunner Books, 2006) p.6

it would help to first ask what keeps us from our calling because we all know that our true hearts get buried.

Spiritual warfare

So many things bury our hearts and cause us to live for lesser pleasures than those that we were actually made for and that will last forever. Obviously *the enemy* of our souls exploits and amplifies our wounds and keeps us locked into a small story, but how many Christian men are taught to engage in spiritual warfare? We are princes and princesses of a Great King and yet we often think and even live like Paupers.

Kris Vallotten states that

> *'Pauperhood is relegated to the children of a lesser god. It is the condition of slaves who have yet to discover their freedom on the other side of the river of baptism and find themselves still captured by the dark prince of tor ture and torment. He is the one who assigns them to a life of poverty, pain and depression through a diabolical play of illusion hoping to conceal their tr ue identity forever. This evil prince feeds his captors the rations of religion to fill their soul's hunger for righteousness...*

> *With three spikes and a thorny crown, the Captain of the Host conquered the devil, eternally disarming his destructive weapons of sin, death, hell and the grave. These were not simply rescued souls to be redeemed, but this was the crowning of the sons who were to be revealed. We are not just soldiers of the cross; we are heirs to the throne.*

His divine nature permeates our souls, transforms our minds, transplants our hearts and transfigures our spirits. We were made to be vessels of His glory and vehicles of His light'. [36]

Individually, the father of lies steals, kills and destroys our true identity and our true destiny. We hear the Echoes from Eden 'Has God really said'? and of the Lords Temptation in the wilderness 'If you are the Son of God' as well as trying to distract him from his mission. We need to know the strategies of the enemy personally, corporately and nationally, it's clear that the enemy has attacked the family in Western culture across the twentieth century and into the first decade of the twenty first. Men and fatherhood in particular have been under demonic assault, it is way overdue that the Church saw this as a spiritual battle against men's calling from God

How has Christianity itself come under attack?

Listen to Os Guiness in his book *The Gravedigger File* about secret papers passed to a Christian in Oxford

'The underlying strategy of Operation Gravedigger is as stark in its simplicity as it is devastating in its results. It may be stated like this: Christianity contributed to the rise of the modern world; the modern world, in turn, undermined Christianity; Christianity has become its own gravedigger. The strategy turns on this monumental irony and the victory we are so close to realising

---

[36] Kris Vallotton, *The Supernatural Ways of Royalty* (Destiny Image Publishers, 2006) p.17-18

> *depends on two elementary insights. First,*
> *that Christianity is now becoming captive to*
> *the very 'modern world' it helped to create.*
> *Second, that our interests are best served,*
> *not by working against the Church, but*
> *by working with it. The more the Church*
> *becomes one with the modern world, the*
> *more it becomes compromised, and the*
> *deeper the grave it digs for itself'* [37]

As he goes onto to say, only one mind is capable of such audacity of vision and sheer force of will, *'For Satan himself transforms himself into an angel of light'* (2 Corinthians 11v14). The Gravedigger File's goal is the complete neutralisation of the modern Western Church by subversion from within. You would have to read The Gravedigger File for yourself to really grasp the three hundred year plan to progressively secularise the Western world. Suffice it to say; if we do not live as though we are at war, we will be 'taken out' from our true calling both individually and as the Body of Christ. Paul says that we are *not* ignorant of the enemy's wiles (strategies, methods).

Fallen powers and our calling

We are heirs to the throne and the divine nature of God does permeate our souls, and God has bestowed on us a great dignity and calling, to be co-workers with him in redeeming creation (1 Corinthians 3v9), but the fact is God's people like all citizens, live in a fallen world, so life can be extremely tough. There is an unseen war and this can also obscure our calling.

R. Paul Stevens states it clearly when he says

---

[37] Os Guiness, *The Gravedigger File* (Hodder and Stoughton, 1983) p.14-15

'The New Testament notes that some superhuman and supernatural beings have fallen (Jude 6; 2 Peter 2v4). Ephesians 6 claims we are engaging these fallen powers as a real factor in our daily existence. Some of these powers have taken on a life of their own, making idolatrous claims on human beings, government, religion, culture, isms, being symbolised by the names and titles that dominate the news (Ephesians 1v21; Galatians 4v8-9). In Ephesians 6 Paul suggests these powers have been colonised (though the term is not used) by Satan himself. The orientation of these powers is parallel to the fall of man and woman' [38]

Stevens goes on to point out that without the eye of faith, these powers can seem omnipotent, but to the eye of faith they are vanquished even though they continue to press their claims and therefore exacerbate the Christian's life and calling in this world. For example, the attack on the family and marriage across the twentieth century and therefore manhood, womanhood, parenthood and so the rearing of children for the next generation, has severely been lost to its original creational design, to be structures of common grace (in creation and redemption) to hold back the evil and the chaos of a fallen world.

Indeed, the frameworks of family, marriage, nation and law are all ordained by God for our good as restraining influences in a fallen world. However, today these creational norms have all been taken over by the ideology of relativism underpinned by secularism, which has no transcendent base, so is deeply humanistic. We must maintain a biblical, creational perspective then of these creational norms as a

---

[38] R. Paul Stevens, *Abolishing the Laity, vocation, work and ministry in a biblical perspective* (Paternoster Press, 1999) p.227

major aspect of our calling but also understand how to live by faith in the overlap of 'this age' and 'the age to come' at the consummation of the Kingdom of God when Jesus returns. This will mean working out to what extent and in what way we feel we need to resist the contemporary 'zeitgeist' (spirit of the age) but in such a way that models the incomparable grace, truth, hope and love that is in Jesus of Nazareth.

The strongholds and Goliaths of modern life are: father absence that stems from the epidemic of societal fatherlessness, secularism with its many related 'isms' like humanism, religious and cultural pluralism, relativism, privatisation, feminism, Capitalism and the worship of work, Individualism and Consumerism. Ministerial professionalism also keeps the majority of men passive and creates a kind of 'spectator Christianity', compounded by the 'sacred-secular' divide within Church culture.

However, there is not a single instance in the New Testament of a person being called to be a religious professional. Obviously many Christians will disagree that some of these 'strongholds' and 'goliaths' are forces that undermine our calling but we must at least have the conversation and be people that think God's thoughts as best we can by his grace and wisdom. Men of Issachar who understood the times in which they lived and knew what Israel should do are needed in this moment (1 Chronicles 12v32).

The vision for God-given manhood has to come from leadership ultimately, so Pastors will have to come to realise *intentional* investment in men is needed. They will need to see that men are the foundation-that historical initiation rites of passage are important to develop substantial masculinity in men who will in turn live out their calling. It's important to evangelise men, but not if you then bring them into an overly feminised environment.

The Tear-fund survey predicts that with the current decline of men, by 2028 men will all but have disappeared from the Church. Pastors have to see then that mentoring and spiritual fathering and investing in men to pursue their calling to leadership is crucial for the future of the Church. Central to the mission of Jesus Christ is to preach the gospel to the poor, heal the broken-hearted, set the captives free, release the prisoners, recovery of sight to the blind, to set at liberty those who are oppressed' (Luke 4v18-19). Are Secularism and Islam winning the battle for the hearts of men?

Work

The over-work culture and the sheer stress of the demands of the workplace today bury our true hearts and keep us in a smaller story than we have been called to. *Work* for example has replaced the basis for how we define ourselves as human beings. Western culture presents men with the illusion of making decisions, but it effectively castrates them from charting a new direction that is beyond and outside the rat race of modern life. *Secularism* that has basically made work sacred leads us to believe that we have no more significant purpose in life than to work.

This is especially the case with the onset of industrialisation and technology, with men in particular; many are so utterly disconnected from the earth, from nature, so disconnected from crucial emotions such as grief, desire or passion. We have been disconnected from the deeply buried wildness that releases healthy sacrificial life giving energy and this has domesticated and sedated so many men. Work is good for creation, for the community, and for us but work is not everything. There is no exaltation of the work of man's hands in the Bible; in fact the exaltation of the work of man's hands is associated with the making of idols (Psalm 115v4; Isaiah 40v18f; 44v9f).

When people think or speak of 'doing the Lord's work' it normally refers to witnessing, evangelism, preaching, or caring for people in some capacity, and it is thought that only this work lasts. R. Paul Stevens says

> 'But the biblical answer to the question 'What is the work of God'? is much more inclusive. The great themes of the Bible are evocative of the work of God. God the creator forms, fabricates, maintains and finishes. God the lover does relational work, bringing dignity, health and meaning. God the saviour does redemptive work, mending, uniting, and saving. God the leader does community-building work and brings things to consummation. Every legitimate human occupation (paid or unpaid) is some dimension of God's own work: making, designing, doing chores, beautifying, organising, helping, bringing dignity, and leading. Here a trinitarian perspective is illuminating. Believers are drawn into the work of God in its fullness' [39]

So the enemy's message to us in our own individual wounds and how he has attacked the Church, combined with how the stress of work damage our hearts – inadvertently through a secularist perspective, are ways that basically bury our hearts, amongst other reasons. Its like a huge stockpile of sorrow has accumulated in the male lineage ever since the coming of the Industrial Revolution.

Moreover, the abandonment of male initiation rites of passage has compounded our disconnection. Consequently, when men feel depressed, lethargic or empty, it's a sign that the primal force inside of us has been put to sleep. Beyond the façade we men hide behind, beyond the myriad of fig

---

[39] R. Paul Stevens, *Abolishing the Laity, vocation, work and ministry in a biblical perspective* (Paternoster Press, 1999) p.118-119

leaves, there is deep longing for meaning, for authenticity, for camaraderie, for real friendship, for true brotherhood and true fatherhood, for battles to fight, to live nobly for a great cause. Martin Luther King said if a man has not found something worth dying for, he's not fit to live. Too strong? Not if you want to live your dream.

So what do we do?

We must be brave enough to face our grief and do whatever it takes to go and get our hearts back. It is time to awake, come out of our various caves and onto the battlefield, but we need mentors or spiritual fathers who have absorbed their pain into a larger vision and meaning, and we need small bands of brothers to be real with. Its starts small, even with two men like Jonathan and his armour bearer who called hundreds of men out of their caves onto the battlefield.

Little platoons.

Jesus started with just twelve men, so he started small and they were a band of brothers. John Eldredge points out that

> 'This is the way of the kingdom of God. Though we are part of a great company, we are meant to live in little platoons. The little companies we form must be small enough for each of the members to know one another as friends and allies. Who will fight for your heart? We hear each other's stories. We discover each other's glories. We learn to walk with God together. We pray for each other's healing. We cover each other's back. This small core fellowship is the essential ingredient for the Christian life. Jesus modelled it for us for a reason. Sure, he spoke to the masses. But he

lived in a little platoon, a small fellowship of friends and allies'. [40]

The true meaning of 'Church' is community (common-unity). It is essentially and most crucially a *shared* life that worships, eats, prays, weeps, laughs, lives, hangs out *together* in each other's homes, just like the first disciples did. Jesus' followers took his example and lived in this way as well (Acts 2v46; 1 Corinthians 16v19; Colossians 4v15). There are over one hundred 'one anothers' in the New Testament, but how do we practice and live those out in meeting once a week for two hours or in a weekly housegroup? It can only really be practiced in a small enough fellowship who are real with each other, and in this relational setting, we can help each other to discover our real desires, our hearts, our calling.

Will the Church see its need of true mentors and spiritual fathers, who will disciple, deeply befriend men and create the kind of environment where core masculine energy is not only affirmed but deeply needed? Jesus has left us a provable model to follow: keep it small, get very real, invest in each other, talk about challenges, adventure, danger, great stories of courage, fighting the giants in our lives, endurance, stories that men can relate to from sports, battle, survival, death and heroic sacrifice, have a vision, know your calling. There is an unseen spiritual war and little platoons of soldiers of Jesus Christ are needed who know the Father intuitively and experientially, like Jonathan who will say to our own Philistine hordes *'Come let us go, it may be that the LORD will work for us. For nothing restrains the LORD from saving by many or by few'.*

---

[40] John Eldredge, *Waking the Dead* (Thomas Nelson, 2003) p.190-1

Jonathan had intimacy with God and very close friends.

Jonathan's heart was surely saturated with such depth and intensity of longing for God, that his relationship with God forged a courage that is incredibly rare. It was a wild outrageous courage that *expected* great things from God, and motivated to do great things for God. He was a masculine kind of man if I can put it that way, a real warrior yet tender. How the modern world is in desperate need of such courageous men who know their God and long to do great exploits for him. Jonathan and his armour bearer basically called men out of their caves onto the battlefield, and despite totally impossible odds against them, God himself joined in and Jonathan lived to tell the story. The story of great courage.

The one thing we can learn from Jonathan and his armour bearer is that the crippling effects of father absence both in society, and the lack of spiritual fathers and mentors in the Church, does not have to define us. His relationship with God surely was the antidote to having an abusive father, and of course in addition to this, he had very close friendships with his armour bearer and of course David, which gives us a model to have a close knit band of brothers, who are down-to-the bone real with each other.

The ferocious, intense, fierce, covenant, unconditional, eternal, indescribably captivating love of Father God that awakens, heals, liberates, realigns and reorients our hearts and shifts our whole being, instils courage. Love gives us courage. Ask the Father to run to us, to show us what his embrace looks like, and we can ask him to initiate us into a deeper more abiding sense of manhood, he will provide for us what we need.

Men have been conditioned to repress their feelings for so long, it is as if we don't know how to express how we really feel. We need to get into the battle to be intentional about pursuing what we feel deeply called to. To come out of the cave we need to get our hearts back.

Where will they bury your heart?

In a sense a calling chooses you, rather than the other way around. This is because the concept of calling is organic to our life journey, but so much depends on how deeply buried our hearts and our deepest core desires are, for as John Eldredge say's 'Your deep desires reveal your deepest calling'. For living our calling is about getting our hearts back.

The story goes that when the British arrived on the shores of Africa to take the body of the missionary David Livingstone back to England, that the local Africans cut the heart out of Livingstone and shouted out 'His body may belong to England, but his heart belongs to Africa'. *If you died tonight, where would they bury your heart?* On top of a T.V. screen, by a computer, a football pitch, at the foot of a Cross? How we answer this question say's a lot about how we define ourselves, and what we are really living for.

A Life-Quest to find our hearts, our desires, our uniqueness.

'You must look at your own longings and aspirations, you must listen to the deep themes of your own life story' Gerald May.

The ways that our hearts get buried means that we can struggle to hear God's voice. In mid-life in particular, a lot of men roll over and are numb, they don't know what they want anymore. I was like that for half my life. When I was shut down to my true heart, I was very numb, but I have also experienced lacerating emotional and physical pain, but give me the pain every time because at least you know something is deeply wrong when you're in pain. When you are numb, you're not even aware of what's wrong. There's deadness, largely because our deep desires have not been met, or our desires have been shamed out of us.

For this reason, most men never really go too deep into their stories and this is so common, not least because of this pathological father wound amongst others. Then the lack of mature, wise mentors and fathers who are able to initiate and facilitate us through our journey so that we don't just live in our heads. This also keeps us stuck in our caves where our hearts just disappear into resignation and we settle for just coping. So we lost the capacity to walk with God.

Because of the effects of stress from the demands of work, Church that tends to be something of a spectator sport for most men, and the fact that there are not too many to help us find our calling, we end up just going through the motions of church life or even praying can become a dead routine. Hence, the modern sedated male. Just like we pick up voicemail messages on our phone, God has left his voicemail messages to us but we may not have picked them up yet for the reasons I have addressed in this book. God's message is there in our memory; it is in our heart, in our story. God's messages then are in our story and our *deep desires* because our desires our us, our uniqueness.

Turning points

One of the ways that can help with getting our hearts back and to confirm what God has put in us as men is to start right where we are, and look at how God has spoken to us in the past. We can do this by looking at as many turning points or 'kairos' moments in our lives as we can think of. A kairos moment is a moment that stops us in our tracks that usually is emotionally charged because of the nature of it.

We all have turning points, and kairos moments in our lives but we can learn from these by observing our reactions, our emotions and thoughts by being very honest with ourselves.

So go back over your life and think of as many turning points that you can think of. Something significant enough that turned us toward life that was affirming and opened our hearts up. Also think of turning points that were so painful that we shut down.

Once we have this list of affirming and painful turning points or kairos moments, then ask yourself: 'Do I see any particular themes here'? 'Are there any messages that may have brought wounds like arrows that lodged in our hearts'? What this does is open us up and it helps to reveal the *why* we got so stuck in a particular way.

However, the kairos moments or turning points that were life giving, enjoyable and the memories that made our hearts come alive – this is where God was trying to communicate to us. This list of affirming and painful turning points gives us a context for looking at our life and this process can be called a life-quest. Next, try to connect all the dots to discern the themes and messages in our lives and this will help us discern how we have made agreements with these messages and how our hearts became so buried and shut down. Now we can interpret the Story of our life.

When we connect with those things and experiences that brought us life and made us feel alive, we connect with the person we really are and where our deep desires are. Human beings cannot tolerate living without any purpose or significance, so when there has been no answer to the *why's* of our life, it is because of *who*, the person we are becoming in the process. We need to connect with the real person we are becoming. When we understand the answer to our *why's*, then we can begin to understand the *what*, in other words, the purpose of our lives as well. This process will also help us know just how much alive we really are, or how alert and oriented we are.

Alert and Oriented Times Three.

In the medical profession, when they are called out to attend to someone who has been injured, the first thing they need to determine is their level of consciousness. They ask: 'Can you tell me your name'? 'Where are you right now'? and 'What day is it'?. If they can answer all three correct, then the person is Alert and Oriented times three. In terms of searching for our calling we also need to be Alert and Oriented times three but to different concepts, namely our Story, our Desires, and our Journey.

Story

It is crucial that we understand the Big Story of the Bible, of Creation, Fall, Redemption and Consummation, in other words the Biblical worldview. We also need to understand our own life story and this is where the above process of a life-quest can help with interpreting our story. In Luke 12v54, 56 they did not know how to interpret 'this present time'. Because they did not understand the story they were living in, they misunderstood who Jesus was and what he was there to do.

When we misunderstand God's Bigger or Upper Story and also own story, then we will not understand our own life.

'Stories don't give answers, but they do offer perspective' said Dan Allender. This is what we need, perspective on our life; orientation to what's going on around us. Story gives us the ability to interpret life. There is so much more to us than we have even begun to imagine, and life is far more than meets the eye, there is always more going on in a much bigger Story which we have also been brought into. So we have to be connected and alert and oriented to both God's Big Story and our own Story.

Desire

Gary Barkalow in his very helpful book *'Its Your Call'* says that

> *'As we walk with God, He will reveal to us His secret about our created design and His intention for us, for our path. But how? Where? What you were created to do is revealed in the form of your desires. As we've already seen, 'it is God who is producing in you both the desire and the ability to do what pleases him' (Phil 2v13 ISV). You see, the really great news is that what you are supposed to do is what you most want to do! I may need to repeat that: What you are supposed to do is what you most want to do! Or as Os Guiness wrote, 'instead of, you are what you do, calling says 'Do what you are''*[41]

If it is true that our deep desires reveal our deepest calling and our desires are in our hearts, then our deepest desires speak loudly about who we really are and our uniqueness. To find our place in God's Story, we have to go to our desires. However, there are different types of desires within us. There are the desires of our flesh that Galatians 5v22 mentions, there are the desires that the enemy seduces us with a desire to satisfy the lusts of our flesh and much more beside; Another source of our desires is from our wounds, in other words we have a desire to self-protect to numb the pain and cover the deep sense of shame, and this is a major source of our desires, it's just that we don't usually see it as a desire.

---

[41] Gary Barkalow, *It's Your Call*, (David C. Cook Publishers, 2010) p.63-4

Then there are the desires from our restored heart, the new heart we have received from God and it is here, that we really need to be connected to. This is why it is crucial to be aware of the defining moments throughout our lives, the memories we have of when we were most alive, what we have dreamt about, the stories we loved as children, the films we love and why, all of these including the painful memories, are meant to bring revelation about who we really are, what we love and why.

Your truest desire becomes your most compelling desire, and what we feel compelled to do speaks volumes about where our true glory lies. Jesus said 'Ask, seek, knock, keep asking, keep seeking, keep knocking'. Dare we desire? What are our desires? However, if there is nothing that we want or desire, then the Lord's words fall on deaf ears, but if you are willing to dig into your life, you will find some hidden treasures…in your heart, in your buried desires.

Frederick Buechner wrote

> *'There is no event so commonplace but that God is present within it, always hiddenly, always leaving you room to recognise him or not to recognise him, but all the more fascinatingly because of that, all the more compellingly and hauntingly….Listen your life. See it for the fathomless mystery that it is. In the boredom and pain of it no less than the excitement and gladness'.*[42]

Obviously life is full of so much mystery. Some people know instinctively what their deep desires or their dreams are, probably because they have had some encouragement and support, but others have not had such help and so they don't even know what their desires are, or are confused

---

[42] Frederick Buechner, *Now and Then* (New York: Harper Collins, 1991) p.87

about even who they are. I have been there. This is why the process of a life-quest where you try to trace the turning points of your life and where God has tried to leave us messages can help us explore and dig and find...our deep desires and what makes us come alive. Mystery though is also an invitation to intimacy with God, because instead of wasting our energy trying to figure out the mysteries of our life, we can allow the mystery to stir us to ask, seek, knock, to cry out to God and rest in his arms until the inner storm calms and we can listen to his voice.

Types of desires that can help us to discover our uniqueness

Think of the desires that have stayed with you throughout your life, in other words, the consistency of your desires, which are historic desires. So we look at the experience of our life and ask 'What have I desired throughout my lifetime'? 'What have I always been interested in'? 'What have I been motivated by'? Although desires come in the moment, these are not really about who we are, they are simply a reaction to something, but our life experience speaks so much more substantially about where our calling lies.

What about the films that moves us? Why do they move us or stir our emotions that resonate with our hearts? Then there are certain words that capture our core desires which our hearts resonate with. For example, write a list of the all the things you have done in the past year that you have really enjoyed doing and then the things that you did not enjoy doing. Then go through each list and ask 'What are the themes or the primary words that describe what I love to bring to any situation or person.

For me, some of those words would be clarity, perspective, focus, encourage, facilitate, and many more. So when we know the specific words that relate and speak of the glory of our life, we can look at a situation and ask 'Are these words or these things required in this job, circumstance or opportunity'. If the job, circumstance or opportunity enables me to do these words that speak of your uniqueness, your glory, then you're probably there for a reason, but if none of who I really am is required, then we're most probably not needed.

Journey

2 Corinthians 3v18 speaks of an ever increasing glory that marks our lives. 'But we all, with unveiled face, beholding as in a mirror the glory of the Lord, are being transformed into the same image from glory to glory, just as by the Spirit of the Lord'. Unveiled, Glory, Transformation, these glorious words are to characterise our lives because this is who God says we really are.

Remember our story began in Genesis 1 when God bestowed on us a glory that we are to reflect, it does not start in Genesis 3. The image of God is being restored in us; we were and are crowned with glory and honour (Psalm 8v5). So God endowed us with a glory so great that all creation pales in comparison, a glory unique to us, just like our fingerprints and the way we laugh is unique to us.

A man deep down wants to know if he has got what it takes to be a man, to be heroic, to be courageous, to be a bold warrior and a woman wants to know that she is beautiful, worth fighting for, worth pursuing and that she is captivating. Why are Christians not characterised and captivated with who they really are both in creation and redemption? Because we have been under a spell, an enchantment that deceived us into believing that being a Christian was about trying not to sin, or going to Church and being nice, or doing the right Christian things, not swearing, not drinking.

Jesus says his core mission was to heal the broken-hearted, set the captives free, restore us to our glory, advance a Kingdom, raise us up to be adopted beloved sons of the Father who are destined to reign with him in the New Jerusalem. When we forget that we are on a journey, we misinterpret our own life and life itself. There is an 'ever-increasingness' then that is to characterise our journey.

Listening

Listening to others is important as well, we need the wisdom and insights of others in our life. As I have said throughout though, without mentors or spiritual fathers, we can stay stuck in our caves, men and women. We need others to ask us questions, to bring clarity about what's going on in our hearts. So a crucial question is 'Who has God brought into my life'?

'What glory/uniqueness did they bring into my life in order to help me with mine'? God will bring key people into our lives to reveal who we really are.

Obviously, we must listen to God, and sometimes the voices of the world, of our own flesh, and especially the lies of the enemy (the defeated one) can sound a lot louder. Hearing his voice depends on building our relationship with him. He is the Living God, and Jesus said that his sheep know his voice, they follow him where he leads us into good pasture, and we his sheep do not listen to the voice of strangers.

His voice becomes the most powerful awakening force because as we choose to believe what he says about us through his Word and Spirit, nothing shakes us, because it is a matter of the Truth of who God says we really are, his Children, his Beloved sons and daughters, Sons and Heirs of the King, Royalty, the Apple of his eye, New Creations, and so much more. As we test what we have heard from God by Scripture and our relational history with him, the inner witness of the Spirit, our circumstances, the counsel of others, in other words, a stable base on which to choose and make decisions, we can proceed confidently within the parameters of our liberty.

We have actually captivated the heart of the King of Glory, why? Because the Fall of man created a cosmic crisis, it launched the greatest rescue campaign in the history of the universe. The Great Eternal King slipped into the enemy's camp as The Ancient of Days disguised as a new-born baby. He literally moved Heaven and Earth to rescue us and raise us up to our true identity and destiny. What does he want from us really? He wants us, everything, our pain, our laughter, tears, our dreams, our fears, all of us, our *heart of hearts*, to bring us into the magnificent epic Story he is still telling, because we all have a crucial role to play in this Epic.

We will need to fight every inch of the way

Because the enemy has assaulted us, actually throughout our lives, first he blinded our minds from knowing the one true living God revealed in Jesus Christ, also he amplified and like a parasite fed on our wounds, and amplified their messages, which we made agreements with to a greater or lesser degree. To the extent that these agreements are still lodged in our hearts, to that extent we will stay stuck in our caves, thinking and believing like paupers instead of princes. I was thinking on Galatians 4v6-7 one day which says that true sons are also heirs of God. I asked Him 'What does it really mean to be an heir of God'? Immediately the answer came 'It means you are royalty', I have bestowed great honour and nobility upon you'. You are a knight; I have embedded this within you'.

Now we are not really used to thinking and believing ourselves to be royalty are we? Carrying our uniqueness, and living out of our true identity and destiny to be kings and priests, beloved sons of the Father, friends of the Most High God, does not just happen automatically. The reason is because we are in a war. However, as Kris Vallotton states in his book *The Supernatural ways of Royalty*

> *'Even if the main people who influenced us were negative role models, as Christians we now follow Christ as our example and hear the Holy Spirit calling us into our true identities. When we begin to act like royalty, issues that felt like mountains in our lives will become mere stepping stones to demonstrate our character…This is tr ue mentality of a prince and princess. They spend more time raising up people around them rather than worr ying about their own significance. They already know who they are inside, which enables them to become selfless and give out more than they receive'.* [43]

Discovery and development of the glory of our life

As we gain clarity about our glory, about what we really have to offer, our uniqueness, another question arises. 'Toward what end, what purpose, what cause'? Many people begin the pursuit of their calling by first looking for a cause. As men, do we not need a cause to give our life to? However, before we start with a cause, we first pursue the discovery and development of the glory of our life, for our life is far bigger than any job, position or even cause. When we are aware and clear about what we have to offer, we can be far more discerning as to what opportunities we are to take and what not to take. So when we are clear about who we are,

---

[43] Kris Vallotton, *The Supernatural Ways of Royalty* (Destiny Image Publishers, 2006) p.74-5

and what we have to offer, we are not as easily manipulated by the needs, predicaments and control of others.

Depending on the extent to which God has awakened us to our core desires, we will be able to that extent be able to pay attention to the conditions of our surroundings. No matter where we live, we will be aware of hundreds and hundreds of *needs*. Whatever unmet needs you feel strong about, you need to listen to that because therein lies your hidden treasure. What needs then have you been awakened to that are not being met? Next, that particular need or needs will develop into a *concern*; you will have deep concern about those needs.

For example, you may read a lot on that topic, or you have a natural tendency toward that topic in conversation. When that need becomes a concern that then develops into a *burden*, where you feel strongly that 'something must be done about this', then it has become a burden, but only the initial stage of a burden. The burden will develop further into 'I must do something about this' and at this point, we are getting near to pinpointing the *cause* we desire to give ourselves to. So the process and development of needs, concerns, burdens can lead us to a cause. It is here where we have to get very specific.

To know what drives us, what we care about, the needs we will want to meet and the cause we will help to conquer, we can ask ourselves questions such as 'What do my dreams and desires drift toward?' What age range or affinity group do I feel led to serve, in other words what particular people group do I have empathy with because of my life experience? What particular needs will I meet? Spiritual needs? Relational, emotional, physical, educational, financial, vocational? Then get more specific by asking *what* are the top two needs I love to meet and *why*? What have I learnt that I could pass on to others?

Finally, what cause or issue makes my heart race? Where could I have the greatest impact for God? How many causes are there, try making an alphabetised list of them. Remember, your deepest desires reveal your deepest calling and out of our brokenness often our calling emerges and is crystallised. So when thinking about our dream, we can ask *'what God- centred dreams can I identify with, that have been buried by life'?*

'What pursuit would release the passion in my life for God?

'What would I attempt to do for God with the rest of my life? Knowing our spiritual gifts, our personalities, our abilities, our temperament, our life experience and what made us come alive are all ways that can give us the clarity we need to pursue our calling, but our hearts needs to have been deeply healed, liberated and awakened.

God gave Elijah two reasons for coming out of the cave.

Elijah was depressed in a wilderness before he crawled into a cave, as far from his calling as he could be. This speaks to our own brokenness, our own desert and our own brokenness, and how God restored Elijah. When we are wounded whether as an isolated incident or we have been stuck for many years, we are like Elijah and go into resignation, we can emotionally and spiritually just give up and even want to die as Elijah did (v4) and thus be far from our calling. In 1 Kings 19v5 Elijah receives his first wake-up call from God. 'Suddenly an angel touched him, and said to him, arise and eat'. But he goes back to sleep again, typical behaviour of a wounded man.

The Life-Quest activity above can help trace our own 'wake-up' calls from God. Have you ever received a wake-up call from God? Think of when the alarm goes off to wake us up in the morning, we usually set it twice. Once to wake us, but we usually just nod off in a kind of in between vague semi- conscious kind of state, before the second alarm call goes off and with this one we must wake up. We would not want to live our lives in this 'in-between vague, semi-conscious' state would we? However, many do live in those 'in between' moments where we have those weird nonsensical dreams that repeat unmercifully, and when we can't find a reason to get up and get going. In these 'in between' moments we can't find a greater purpose than getting a little more sleep and staying warm. Being stirred up, awakened, roused, excited is meant to be the condition of our heart, as we live as a co-worker with God.

He receives a second wake-up call in v7. *'And the angel of the LORD came back the second time, and touched him, and said, 'arise and eat, because the journey is too great for you'.* Elijah is exhausted though, he thinks he is alone, marginalised, and many people feel like that today with the demands from work that has taken over so much of our lives in Western culture. Elijah gets up and goes into a cave. God comes to him and speaks to him in a way he had not known before, in a tender and gentle voice.

The wind, earthquake and the fire all passed by and God's voice was not in them, he then heard a still, small voice and it was hearing God's voice in new way preceded the modifying of his original calling. After asking 'What are you doing here Elijah'? The still, small voice of God was greater than the earthquake, wind and fire and it awakened, revived, energised and mobilised him.

Then comes the two reasons God gives him for coming out of the cave. In verse 15 God says 'Go, return. Then in verse 16 God says anoint two kings. Basically, God says to Elijah *'Go back to the calling I originally gave you'* and the second reason God effectively say's to him *'Be a mentor to a younger man'* (Elisha). This is what men need, a calling from God, a cause, and to be prepared to be a mentor in the right season as God leads us.

We all have a unique spiritual DNA and the seed that has been planted within us by God will also birth what he has planted within us. The seed is the uniqueness of how God has gifted, stirred, equipped and called us. The stirring of his Spirit is what we need to connect to and so it becomes crucial to train ourselves to hear God's voice. It takes a season to receive enough healing and enter new levels of wild freedom, to know *experientially* in our spirit, our hearts and mind to be transformed so that we actually, literally think, believe and behave from the new heart that God has put in us.

It can feel like a scary journey actually to discover the deep desires in our hearts, because we will need to go through the many barriers and lies that have become strongholds in our minds and hearts, like our need for approval, fear of rejection, inability to trust, the courage it takes to risk going into our buried hearts for fear of just more disappointment.

It will mean for some entering into our brokenness instead of settling for mere survival and coping mechanisms, for God has called us into a magnificent epic Story and we have a crucial role to play. Remember, it is out of your brokenness that you discover what you have to offer others, but this is why men especially, need the close friendships that Jonathan had with David and his armour bearer, because we give each other the necessary energy, vulnerability, outlet, transparency and sharpness that we need to live in a bigger Story – God's Story. We cover each other's back and fight for each other, we are real with our stories and help each other discover the glory that is in us.

Again Gary Barkalow is very helpful here

> 'You see, your calling or glor y is in you. It's not something you go get, like a degree, position or title. It's already written in your life, though it can and must be developed. Your glory compels you to do something in every situation, a compulsion that you can

*choose to go with, hold back from, or ignore. It
is what your heart almost always sees, knows,
notices, wants to do, or is burdened by. Your
glory is written on your heart, and you must
go there to discover and understand it'* [44]

In the final analysis, when all is said and done, it all
comes down to this *'What kind of a man do you really want
to be?* Like the six hundred hiding in caves or like Jonathan
and his armour bearer?

---

[44] Gary Barkalow, *Its Your Call*, (David C. Cook Publishers, 2010) p.85

SMALL GROUP CALLING MEN OUT OF THE CAVE COURSE

CHAPTER 1: 'THEY WERE HIDING IN CAVES'

Read 1 Samuel 13v5-6

Reflect and discuss:

1. Are there impossible odds against you as an individual or against the Church in the culture in which you live- if so, what do you think they are they?
2. In what ways do you or the Church face danger from the enemy?
3. 'The people hid in caves, in rocks, in holes, in pits'…. How are you still hiding from facing your deepest fears? How is the church still hiding?

Apply: In areas where you may still be 'hiding'- how can you come out of hiding?
>Optional for further discussion: DVD Clip: Scene 13 The Full Monty

Read 1 Samuel 14v1, 6-7, 12-15, 39, 43-44

Reflect and discuss:

1. Jonathan had an abusive father yet he was a man of great courage.
   How did your father fail you or how did he offer strong masculine energy?

What role model for manhood did you have before you were 20 and what did it look like?

2. In what areas of your life are you willing to say 'Come let us go, it may be that the LORD will work for us, for nothing restrains the LORD from saving by many or by few'?

3. His armour bearer was willing to take the huge risk against impossible odds- Do you have a friend close enough who will fight for your heart and stand with you in pursuing your dream?

Apply: Where in particular are you willing to face the odds stacked against you and say 'It may be that the LORD will work for me/us'

>Optional for further discussion: DVD Clip: Scene 5-8 Coach Carter

CHAPTER 2. 'UNDER A SPELL'

Read 2 Corinthians 10v3-5

Reflect and discuss:

1. In what ways do you think that Secularism has enchanted Christian men and caused us to forget our true calling and identity in Christ?
2. Do you have a view that only those in 'full time' Christian work are the only ones who are engaged with ministry?
3. In what ways are men leading in your church so that you experience authentic koinonia- a sharing of your whole life?

Apply:

How can you live out Gospel and Community in practice so that we are not under the spell of a 'Sacred-Secular' mind-set >Optional for further discussion: DVD Clip: Scene at beginning of film American Beauty 'This is my life scene'. (Q1) The Modern sedate male.

Read: 2 Corinthians 4v3-4

Reflect and Discuss:

1. The person on the street believes in millions or billions of years of evolution. How has this blinded their minds and put them 'under a spell' of the father of lies?
2. If NT ministry simply means service, how can the local church equip people for ministry in the home, the school, college, workplace, neighbourhood, community and other spheres of influence?

3. Paul said in 1 Thessalonians 2v8 that the gospel and 'our own lives' are inseparable. How are you living out the gospel so that you are sharing your whole lives with others?

Apply: >Optional for further discussion: DVD Clip: Scene X1 Time: 01:21:09 to 01:25 Gladiator. Men under pressure need to 'Come together as one, lock their shields of faith tight together. Men who suffer and fight together forge a camaraderie and brotherhood

CHAPTER 3. 'HISTORICAL AND SOCIAL REASONS FOR FATHER ABSENCE'

Read Luke 4v1-13

Reflect and discuss:

1. How has God 'Initiated' you by leading or driving you into your own wilderness experience?
2. In what ways do you think we live in a fatherless society?
3. How in particular do you and your church live as though you are at war-or not?

Apply:

How can you be a spiritual father or a mentor to a younger man.

Optional for further discussion: DVD Clip: Scene 4 The Kingdom of Heaven

It is crucial for a father to initiate his son into manhood.

Read: Genesis 32 Jacob wrestling with the Angel.

Reflect and Discuss:

1. How have you wrestled with God in the dark alone-why, how?
2. Jacob wrestled until he was weakened-then he clung to God- In what ways has God broken your own independence and self-sufficiency?
3. He wrestled 'Until the Breaking of the Day'. Are you still wrestling, or clinging?

Apply: How can you make a difference in a younger man's life?

>Optional for further discussion: DVD Clip: Boyz in the Hood Father and Son scene

We wrestle with our own manhood issues more if we have not been fathered or mentored well.

CHAPTER 4- 'MEN CALLED TO BE THE FOUNDATION'

Read Ephesians 6v1-4

Reflect and discuss:

1. Did your father provoke you to anger or did he train you- explain how he did or did not do both
2. Myles Munroe says the following terms describe God's purpose for a man rather than roles: visionary, leader, teacher, cultivator, provider and protector. What do you think? How many of these are you living out as a man and in what ways?
3. God planned everything before He began to create, he did not make it up as he went along. So He begins to build the human race by placing the man at the bottom of the entire building-to be the foundation (Genesis 2v15). God laid the foundation first and this is the priority in building, you have to start with a strong foundation.

This implies that a society is only as good as its men- <u>Discuss whether you agree or disagree.</u>

Apply: In what ways can you begin to be a visionary, a leader, a teacher, a cultivator, a provider and a protector? >Optional for further discussion: DVD Clip: Speech in Last Scene in Courageous

Read: 2 Timothy 1v2 and 2v1-6

Reflect and Discuss:

1. Has your own father or another father figure ever referred to you as 'my beloved son' and what do you believe it means?

2. 2v2 provides a fourfold mentoring model. Who has been a true mentor to you and who is now?

3. Paul gives the images of soldier, athlete and farmer to describe examples of discipleship. What strong Christ-like men have stood alongside you as you 'endured hardship as a good soldier of Jesus Christ'?

Apply: Get alongside another man and begin to pray into the one area that may entangle you and so begin to disentangle yourself from the 'affairs of this life'.

Optional for further discussion: DVD Clip Braveheart: Scene where Wallace implores the heir to the throne of Scotland, Robert the Bruce 'if you would just lead, they would follow'. Men need to be leaders in all areas of life.

CHAPTER 5- FATHER ABSENCE

Read Genesis 32v24-30 and Hosea 12v4

Reflect and discuss:

1. Has God ever *initiated* you into a deeper more substantial manhood-how?
2. Describe a time in your life when you were led into a wilderness experience-did you 'wrestle with tears' like Jacob?
3. What particular experiences has God used to cause you to 'cling' to Him and cry 'I will not let you go until you bless me'?

Apply: In what areas of your life can you wield the Sword of Truth (The Word) in what feels like a desert time

Optional for further discussion: DVD Clip: Braveheart: Scene between Father and son on battlefield 'I've lived to become proud of the man you have become'.

Read: 2 Samuel 14v23-15v1-6

Reflect and Discuss:

1. In 14v23 David did not want to see his son- How did this affect Absalom?
2. In 14v28 Absalom dwelt two full years in Jerusalem but did not see the king's face- what do you think is happening in Absalom's heart?
3. In 15v6 Absalom 'stole the hearts of the men of Israel'- What is happening in this father-son relationship?

Apply: Is there area that needs reconciliation between you and your father? How can you initiate the process as a son or as a father?

>Optional for further discussion: DVD Clip: Gladiator. Scene: Between Father and son: 'You shall not be the next emperor'- the son lets out agonising cry 'If only you had loved me' then strangles his father and becomes a murderous tyrant.

The Father wound is deeper than we have acknowledged. We must face our own denial

CHAPTER 6- 'BECOMING THE BELOVED OF GOD THROUGH THE FATHER'S EMBRACE'

Read 1 John 4v18 and Luke 15v20-22

Reflect and Discuss:

1. Explain: In what ways in particular has God delivered you from fear?
2. Are you living in the reality of having received all three gifts from the Father's Embrace- The Robe of Righteousness; The Ring of the Authority of son- ship; and the Shoes of Freedom?
3. Are you settling for being a servant or do you know in your heart that you are a true son?

Apply: Is there an individual you know who struggles to trust God who you can minister the love of God to?

>Optional for further discussion: DVD Clip: Good Will Hunting- Scene: Last scene in Robin Williams' office 'It's not your fault' as he hands him his case history- he weeps and something is shifted- he goes onto to pursue the woman.

Read: Matthew 8v1-3 and John 14v9-10

Reflect and Discuss:

1. After preaching the Sermon on the Mount- a leper pushed through the crowd to get to Jesus and He reached out to touch him- Has Jesus ever reached out to touch an area of your life that feels 'untouchable'?
2. The leper would have felt like a marginalised outcast- so how did this staggering gesture from the Lord affect him?

3. Jesus said that the kingdom of heaven suffers violence and the violent take it by force-Do you think this leper took the kingdom of heaven by force? How?

Apply: How can you reach out and touch a person who may feel such a marginalised outcast as the leper?

>Optional for further discussion: DVD Clip Les Miserables' Scene: When the police bring him back to the priest's house because he has stolen some silver and the priest gives him even more.....

CHAPTER 7: FINDING AND LIVING YOUR CALLING.

Read Proverbs 16v32; Luke 4v1-15

Reflect and Discuss:

1. In what ways do you rule your own spirit and anger-so that you are able to offer the man God is forging you into for others?
2. Describe a season in the wilderness where God developed a 'warrior- spirit' into you to fight the enemy?
3. In what particular ways have you emerged out of your own desert and are ready to be a king with a vision bigger than yourself and a warrior who fights for the truth in the areas of your life?

Apply:

In what ways are you are fighting to pursue the vision and calling that God has put within your heart?

Optional for further discussion: DVD Clip: Braveheart: Scene: William Wallace's speech to his countrymen before the go into battle against a much larger English army.

The Fight for Freedom is crucial.

Read: 2 Corinthians 3v18; Luke 12v54-56; 1 Kings 19

Reflect and Discuss:

1. Unveiled, Glory, Transformation- How in particular are you experiencing these powerful words that are to characterise our lives?

2. In the Luke passage they did not really understand who Jesus really was because they did not understand God's Big Story they were living in. How have you connected with God's Big Story and how are you living it out in particular?

3. In v5 of 1 Kings 19 Elijah receives his first 'wake up' call. In v7 he receives his second 'wake up' call. Then God gives him two reasons for coming out of the cave. First, 'Go, return'. Second 'Anoint two kings and be a mentor to a younger man' (Elisha).

God basically said to Elijah 'Go back to the original calling I gave you and be a mentor to a younger man'.

Describe any 'wake up' calls you have received from God. Are you far away from living out your sense of calling, or have you heard the voice of God saying to you 'Go'?

Apply:

How can you 'wake up' from being stuck in your own wilderness and connect to what God has put into your heart-so that you can live from your heart's calling from God?

Optional for further discussion: DVD Clip: A Few Good Men Courtroom scene 'You can't handle the truth'/Code Red.

We need to offer the Truth of who we really are in Jesus

For further information

For further information on this book or to contact
Nigel, please email: resistzeitgeist807@gmail.com